Contents

What's in it for you?   7
About this Handbook

The Alpine/Solara Family   8
Main production dates and changes

Road Test Data   10
Performance figures from *Autocar*

In the Driving Seat   11
Instruments, controls, layout

Filling Station Facts   22
Garage forecourt guide to tyre pressures etc.

QUICK CHECK CHART   25
Fill-up data at-a-glance

In an Emergency   26
Get-you-home kit, wheel changing, towing, light bulb renewal

Save It!   36
Cutting motoring costs — safely

Vital Statistics   41
Technical data on all models

Tools for the Job   49
Getting equipped — what to buy

Service Scene   52
What to do, when and how to do it

Body Beautiful   83
Cleaning, renovating, repairing bodywork

The Personal Touch   89
Adding accessories

Troubleshooting   98
Charts to help when things go wrong

Car Jargon Explained   110
'What are they talking about. . .?'

Conversion Factors   118
'What's that in pounds per square inch. . . .?'

Index   120

1978 model Alpine GLS

1982 model Alpine SX

1981 model Solara GLS

6

What's in it for You?

Whether you've bought the book yourself, or had it given to you, the idea was probably the same in either case - to help you get the best out of your Alpine or Solara and perhaps to make your motoring a bit less of a drain on your hard-earned cash at the same time.

Garage labour charges can easily be several times your own hourly rate of pay, and usually form the main part of any servicing bill; we'll help you avoid them by carrying out the routine services yourself. Even if you don't want to do the regular servicing, and prefer to leave it to your Talbot dealer, there are some things you should check regularly just to make sure that your car's not a danger to you or anyone else on the road; we tell you what they are.

If you're about to start doing your own servicing (whether to cut costs or to be sure that it's done properly), we think you'll find the procedures described give an easy-to-follow introduction to what can be a very satisfying way of spending a few hours of your spare time.

We've included some tips that should save you some money when buying replacement parts and even while you're driving; there's a chapter on cleaning and renovating your car, and another on fitting accessories.

Apart from the things every owner needs to know to deal with mishaps like a puncture or a blown bulb, we've put together some Troubleshooter Charts to cover the more likely problems that can crop up with even the most carefully maintained car sooner or later.

There's also a set of conversion tables and a comprehensive alphabetical index to help you find your way round the book.

If the bug gets you, and you're keen to tackle some of the more advanced repair jobs on your car, then you'll need our Owner's Workshop Manual for the Alpine and Solara which gives a step-by-step guide to all the repair and overhaul tasks, with plenty of illustrations to make things even clearer.

H.12292

The Alpine/Solara Family

Introduced to the U.K. in 1976, the Chrysler Alpine (as it was then called) received great acclaim from the motoring press and public alike, and in the same year won the Car of the Year Award. The Alpine name has long been familiar to the motoring public, but this transverse engined hatchback with front wheel drive represented a giant step forward. The first models available were the GL, with a 1294 cc engine, and the S with a 1442 cc. Towards the end of 1976 they were joined by the GLS, which was mechanically identical to the S but boasted electric windows and a generally higher level of trim.

Mechanical improvements to the range in 1977 and 1978 included the provision of warning lights for choke, handbrake and brake pad wear. Rear wash/wipe was optional on the GL and standard on the other models.

Various improvements to internal and external trim, including a vinyl roof on the GLS, occurred during this period. The 1442 cc engine was made available as an option on the GL from September 1977.

In December 1978 the LS 1.3 and 1.6 models became available. The GL model specification was improved to include halogen headlamps, and the S model was discontinued, being effectively replaced by the GL with the larger engine option.

A couple of 'special edition' models were available in 1979. April saw the Sunseeker Saloon, based on the larger-engined GL and sporting tinted glass, a sunroof, alloy wheels and a distinctive black paint job. The GLS Special, introduced in June, had power-assisted steering as well as tinted glass and a sunroof.

All models benefited from a face-lift at the beginning of 1980. The front end of the car was redesigned, whilst inside a new facia layout and new style interior trim were seen. A new 'top of the range' model, the SX Saloon, also made its appearance. The SX was powered by a 1592 cc engine and was at first only available with automatic transmission. It was equipped with advanced technology features such as a trip computer, cruise control, digital clock and headlamp washers. Externally it was distinguished by a vinyl roof and bronze tinted glass. The Talbot name

had now replaced that of Chrysler.

The Solara joined the family in April 1980. Mechanically the same as the Alpine, all models have four doors and a separate boot. Models available initially were the LS 1.3, with the 1294 cc engine, and the LS 1.6, GL, GLS and SX, all with the 1592 cc engine. As with the Alpine, the SX version was only available with automatic transmission and was comprehensively equipped. A 5-speed manual gearbox was a possible option on the GLS; this option was extended to SX purchases (both Alpine and Solara) early in 1981.

In September 1981, further improvements were made to the Alpine/Solara range, the most significant being to increase engine performance and fuel economy. The Alpine GL was given the 1592 cc engine already fitted to its Solara counterpart. Both GL models were available with the 5-speed manual gearbox option, and the 5-speed box became standard equipment on the GLS models.

Two more 'special editions' brightened up the range in 1982, namely the Alpine Arrow in March and the Solara Sceptre in May. Series 2 models, including the LE 1.3 and 1.6, made their appearance in October 1982, and a 1.3 version of the GL could be obtained in both body styles. The 1442 cc engine was phased out by the end of the year, and the 5-speed gearbox became standard issue for all 1.6 models.

Specification details are given in *Vital Statistics*, but here is a summary of the main production dates and changes:

January 1976	Alpine range introduced to UK - GL (1294 cc) and S (1442 cc)
September 1976	Alpine GLS added to range - as S with extras
September 1977	Extra warning lights, new interior trim, 1442 cc engine available on GL. Rear wash/wipe on standard S and GLS
October 1978	Diagnostic checking facility and brake fluid level warning lamp added
December 1978	LS available, 1294 cc or 1442 cc. GL specification improved, S discontinued
April 1979	Sunseeker Saloon (special edition based on 1442 cc GL) available
June 1979	GLS Special Saloon available, with power steering
January 1980	SX introduced - 1592 cc, automatic transmission, power steering, comprehensively equipped. All models have new-look front end and redesigned interior trim
April 1980	Solara range introduced - LS 1.3 (1294 cc), LS 1.6, GL, GLS and SX (all 1592 cc)
March 1981	5-speed manual gearbox available on all SX models
September 1981	Engine modifications for improved power and economy. Alpine GL now with 1592 cc engine. 5-speed gearbox standard on all GLS models, optional on GL
March 1982	Limited edition Alpine Arrow (1592 cc) available
May 1982	Special edition Solara Sceptre (1592 cc) available
September 1982	1442 cc engine discontinued
October 1982	Economy models LE 1.3 and 1.6 (both Alpine and Solara) introduced; Series 2 begins
December 1982	5-speed gearbox standard on all 1.6 models.

Road Test Data taken from

The figures published here are extracts from *Autocar* magazine road tests.

Fuel consumption: The mpg figure is the overall consumption figure for their test period, including performance testing. Many owners will achieve significantly better consumption figures. The formula on the right provides a guide ('**mpg**' refers to the quoted overall test figure).

	Alpine GL	Alpine S	Alpine GLS	Alpine SX (auto)	Solara GLS
Maximum speed (mph)	90	101	99	94	95
Overall fuel consumption (mpg)	29.2	29.3	27.7	27.5	29.0
Fuel consumption (mpg) at constant:					
30 mph	52.5	49.4	49.4	34.3	53.5
50 mph	38.8	37.7	37.7	37.1	50.0
70 mph	27.8	29.4	29.4	28.7	30.8
Range on full fuel tank (miles)	374	375	355	352	371
Acceleration (seconds):					
0–30 mph	4.4	3.9	3.7	5.6	3.5
0–40 mph	7.5	6.4	6.2	8.0	5.8
0–50 mph	11.3	9.0	8.6	11.5	8.1
0–60 mph	16.9	13.3	12.6	15.8	12.0
0–70 mph	24.6	18.6	17.2	21.7	17.0
Standing start ¼ mile	20.5	19.3	18.9	20.4	18.5
40–60 mph in normal top gear	14.8	11.8	10.8	12.0	14.2

Driving conditions guide

Driving style	Driving conditions		
	severe	average	easy
	−10%		+10%
Hard	mpg	mpg	
Average	+10%	+20%	+30%
Gentle	+20%	+30%	

Four-dial instrument panel – later type

1 Handbrake on/low brake
   fluid level warning light
2 Oil pressure/oil level
   warning light
3 'Lights on' warning light
4 Direction indicator warning
   light

5 Main beam warning light
6 No charge warning light
7 Low fuel level warning light
8 Fuel gauge

9 Speedometer
10 Trip meter reset knob
11 Clock
12 Temperature gauge

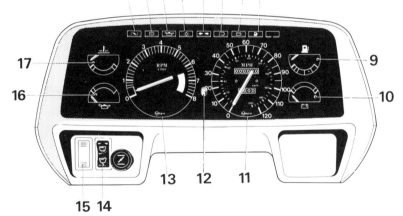

Six-dial instrument panel – later type

1 Choke warning light
2 Handbrake on/low brake
   fluid level warning light
3 Oil pressure/oil level
   warning light
4 'Lights on' warning light
5 Direction indicator warning
   light

6 Main beam warning light
7 No charge warning light
8 Low fuel level warning light
9 Fuel gauge
10 Voltmeter
11 Speedometer

12 Trip meter reset knob
13 Tachometer
14 Rear wash/wipe switch
15 Panel light dimmer
16 Oil pressure gauge
17 Temperature gauge

Fuel gauge

The fuel gauge will only give an accurate reading when the car is on level ground and the ignition has been switched on for a few seconds. Always refill the tank before the fuel gauge reads empty, especially if the car is new to you and you don't know how accurate the gauge is!

Temperature gauge

With the engine cold, the temperature gauge will read in the left-hand segment; once the engine has warmed up, it should read somewhere in the centre segment. If at any time the needle enters the red zone, the engine is overheating and you must stop and investigate the cause. (See *Filling Station Facts* for how to top up the cooling system, and *Troubleshooting* for likely causes of overheating.)

Oil pressure gauge

This gauge is fitted to some models in addition to the oil pressure warning light. The gauge must indicate above the red segment when the engine is running. If it reads low, check the oil level and top up if necessary. If this doesn't restore the oil pressure, **don't** drive the car until the problem has been corrected. It might just be a faulty gauge, but if the oil pressure really is low you can cause serious damage to the engine by running it in this state.

Voltmeter

This instrument indicates battery voltage when the ignition is switched on. With the engine running above idle speed, the needle should indicate in the centre zone. Readings in the extreme left (low voltage) or right (high voltage) suggest that the battery is being under- or over-charged. If a quick check of the alternator drivebelt and wiring connectors doesn't reveal the cause, take the car to a Talbot dealer or automobile electrician to have the charging system checked.

Tachometer (rev counter)

The tachometer shows engine speed in revs per minute (rpm). Experience will tell you at what speeds the engine is most economical. Always change up a gear before the needle enters the red zone, otherwise damage due to over-revving may result.

Instrument panel warning lights

Most of the warning lights are self-explanatory once you know what the symbols mean. Some of them require you to take some action, so let's consider them briefly.

Choke warning light

If your car's equipped with this light, it's to remind you that the choke control is pulled out. You shouldn't need to drive more than a mile or so with the choke out, even in winter — otherwise you're wasting fuel and maybe damaging the engine too. The light should go out when the choke control is pushed home.

Brake warning light

On early models this light has a little handbrake symbol on it, and serves to remind the driver that the handbrake is applied. On later models the symbol is changed to a circle with an exclamation mark in the middle, and the light will illuminate not only if the handbrake is applied, but also if there is a fault in the braking system. If this type of light comes on with the handbrake off, stop at once and investigate the brake fluid level. Top up if necessary and keep a close eye on the level in future — you may have a leak in the braking system, which is obviously something to put right without delay. If the level is OK, drive on carefully and have the braking system checked professionally at the first opportunity.

Oil pressure/oil level warning light

This light should come on when you turn the ignition on before starting the engine. (If not, the bulb may have blown, or the oil pressure switch or wiring may be faulty.) It should go out as soon as the engine starts, and stay out all the time that the engine is running. If it ever comes on whilst you're driving along, *stop at once* and check the oil level. Maybe it only needs topping up, in which case do so and resolve to keep a closer eye on the level in future, but if the level is OK and the oil pressure is low, you could ruin the engine in a very short time by driving on. **Don't** drive the car with the oil pressure warning light on, unless you are satisfied that the oil pressure is normal and the light itself is faulty. Telephone the nearest Talbot garage for advice if in doubt.

On later Alpine and all Solara models the oil pressure warning light also serves to indicate if the oil level is low when the engine is started. If the light keeps flashing after starting the engine, the oil level is low. Check the level using the dipstick and top up as necessary. If the car is standing on a slope when the engine is started, it's possible for a false low reading to result. In that case, stop the engine when the car is standing on level ground, wait a moment for the oil to return to the sump and restart the engine.

It's a good idea to check the oil level periodically using the dipstick in any case, especially if you're about to set off on a long journey, since a low oil level will not be indicated by the warning light once the engine is running.

No charge warning light

Like the oil pressure warning light, this light should illuminate with the ignition on and the engine stationary, and go out as soon as the engine starts. If it comes on with the engine running — apart maybe from flickering at idle — it means that the battery's not charging. Stop as soon as convenient and check the alternator drivebelt and wiring connections. If these are OK, you can get quite a long way on the juice available from a healthy battery, provided you don't use the lights or starter too much. You'll have to get the charging system seen to without delay, though, or you'll end up with a flat battery. If the alternator drivebelt is broken or loose, fix it before you go any further (see *Service Scene*), otherwise the engine will overheat.

Low fuel warning light

The low fuel light will start to flash as the level in the tank gets low. When it comes on continuously, you've only got a gallon or so left in the fuel tank, so stop and fill up without delay.

Switches

Ignition switch/steering lock

This combination unit has four or five positions, according to type. Reading clockwise from the first position, the functions are as follows:

S (Stop): *Ignition off, accessories off. The steering lock will engage if the key is withdrawn*
A (Accessories): *Ignition off, accessories (radio, heater blower etc.) on, steering unlocked*
G (Garage): *Ignition off, accessories off, steering unlocked. Not all units have this position*
M (Marche): *Ignition on, accessories on, steering unlocked. This is the normal running position*
D (Demarreur): *Ignition on, starter motor operating. The key automatically returns to positon 'M' when released*

A couple of points are worth noting. First, if you have difficulty in inserting or removing the key in position 'S', try rotating the steering wheel slightly to relieve the tension on the lock. Never turn the key to position 'S', or try to remove it, while the car is moving. Secondly, remember that if you leave the key in position 'A', items such as the heater blower and radio can be drawing current from the battery — so don't leave the car unattended with the key in this position.

It's an excellent idea to record the ignition key serial number and to carry it with you (outside the car!)

Ignition switch/steering lock positions. See text for explanation

at all times. You'll never know how useful this can be until you lose a key!

Windscreen wiper/washer control

The windscreen wiper switch is controlled by the stalk coming out of the right-hand side of the steering column cowl. Its functions are explained in the accompanying illustration. The windscreen washer is operated by pulling the level towards the steering wheel. If headlamp washers are fitted, they will operate whenever the windscreen washer is used if the lights are switched on.

Lighting/horn switch

This is controlled by the longer stalk on the left-hand side of the steering column cowl. With the switch knob in position 'O', the lights are off. Move the switch to position '1' and the sidelights are on with the lever in the upper position, plus dipped beam headlights if it is moved to the lower position. In position '2', main beam headlights are lit with the lever in the lower position, and dipped beam in the upper position.

Pulling the lever towards the steering wheel causes the headlamps to flash; pushing the end of the knob inwards will sound the horn.

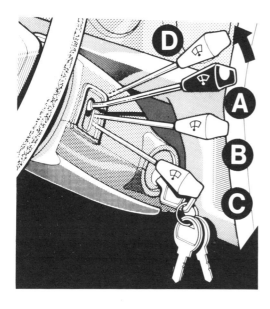

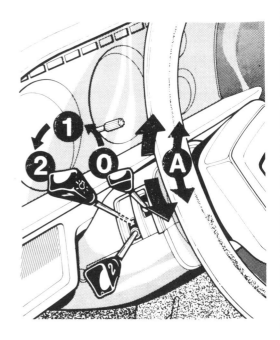

Windscreen wiper and washer control

A   *Off*
B   *Low speed*
C   *High speed*
D   *Flick wipe (high speed)*

Lighting and direction indicator switches

0   *Lights off*
1   *Sidelights/dipped beam*
2   *Dipped beam/main beam*
A   *'Lane change' position for direction indicators*

Direction indicator switch

This is the shorter stalk on the left-hand side. Move the lever upwards to signal a right turn, downwards for a left turn. If the dashboard warning light fails to flash when you signal a turn, either a bulb has blown or some other fault has developed.

Facia switches

These switches are of the 'push-push' type, ie pushing the switch once will turn it on, pushing it again will turn it off. According to model and year, they control some or all of the following:

Rear fog lamps. These will only operate when the headlamps are on dipped beam. Don't forget to turn the fog lamps off when conditions become clearer, or you may dazzle following traffic.

Heated rear window. Very useful for clearing mist or ice from the rear window, but don't leave it switched on longer than necessary (or with the engine switched off) as it draws a high current from the battery.

Hazard warning switch. Causes all four indicator lights to flash in unison. The use of this switch is only permitted when the car is stationary. Contrary to popular belief, use of the hazard warning signal does not entitle the driver to park on double yellow lines!

Brake pad wear light and test switch. Fitted to later models, this light will illuminate during braking if any of the front brake pads is worn to the point where renewal is necessary. You can test the warning light bulb by pressing the test switch (ignition on). If the warning light comes on when braking, check the pads without delay (see *Service Scene*). Don't neglect regular checks of the brake pads just because the light hasn't come on though!

Other switches

According to model and year, your car may have switches for extras such as rear wash/wipe, electrically operated windows, etc. Operation of these switches is self-explanatory. If you're lucky enough to have electric windows fitted to your car, remember that they are quite powerful and can make a nasty impression on fingers or other objects obstructing their movement!

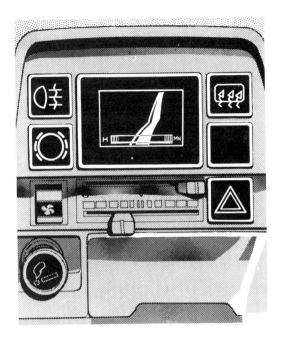

Typical facia switch layout. See symbol chart for switch application

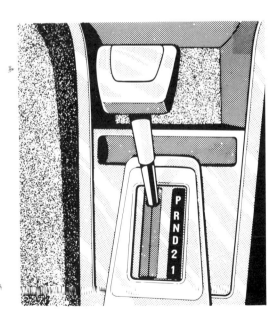

Automatic transmission selector positions

Automatic transmission

Vehicles equipped with automatic transmission also have an automatic choke. When starting the engine from cold, don't touch the throttle peddle – the choke will adjust the engine speed as the engine warms up. Remember that the starter motor will only operate with the transmission selector in 'P' or 'N'. Apply the footbrake before engaging a drive range in case the car lurches forwards or backwards.

The functions of the selector positions are as follows:

P (Park): *Transmission is locked, engine can be started. Do not engage 'P' while moving, or damage may result*

R (Reverse): *Press the button in the lever when engaging reverse. Do not engage while the car is moving forwards*

N (Neutral): *No gears engaged, transmission is unlocked. Engine can be started. Select 'N' when idling in traffic*

D (Drive): *Normal driving. Fully automatic selection of all gears*

2 (Second): *Only first and second gears will be engaged. Useful when engine braking is required. Do not select '2' at speeds above 68 mph. The button must be pressed when engaging*

1 (First): *If engaged from rest, the transmission will not move out of first gear, if engaged at speed, it will change down to first when speed is low enough. Again, the button must be pressed when engaging, and speed must be below 68 mph.*

The speeds at which gearchanging take place when 'D' is selected will depend on load and throttle position. At wide throttle openings the change speeds will be higher. For maximum acceleration, the 'kickdown' facility will cause the transmission to change down (if speed is not too high) when the throttle pedal is pressed to the floor. This is not recommended from the point of view of economy though!

You cannot start a vehicle with automatic transmission by towing or pushing – so it's a good idea to carry a pair of jump leads in case you get stuck with a flat battery. If the car breaks down and needs towing, it must be towed no faster than 25 mph and no further than 15 miles, otherwise serious transmission damage may result. If the breakdown is due to a transmission fault, the car may only be towed with the front wheels raised off the ground (suspended tow).

17

Effect of throttle pedal position on automatic transmission change speeds

1   *Gentle driving – low-speed changes*
2   *Harder driving – high-speed changes*
3   *Kickdown – maximum speed changes*

Heating and ventilation controls

These are best understood by studying the diagram. It is possible to obtain almost any desired combination of heated and fresh air. Use the booster fan when output is insufficient with the car stationary or travelling at low speeds.

If heater output is insufficient in winter, it may be that the engine thermostat is faulty or missing.

Optional extras

Cruise control

Fitted as original equipment on SX models with automatic transmission, the cruise control enables the driver to maintain a constant speed without touching the throttle, regardless of hills, headwinds etc. Motorways or similar roads are obviously the best places to use this gadget – you should resume full control yourself in heavy traffic or in unfavourable weather conditions.

To engage the control, move the slide switch to

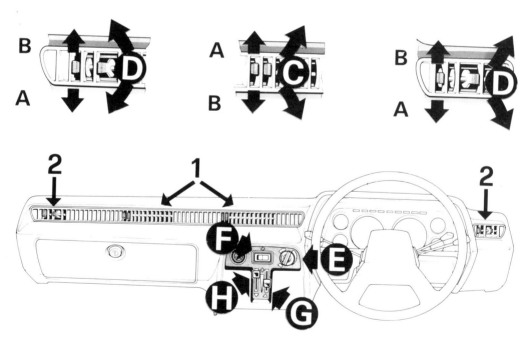

Typical heating and ventilation controls

A	Closed	D	Direction control	G	Screen airflow control
B	Open	E	Temperature control	H	Interior airflow control
C	Direction control	F	Fan control	1	Fresh air vents
				2	Heater-controlled vents

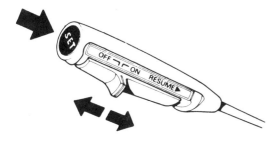

Cruise control switch

the slide switch is moved to the 'OFF' position, or when the ignition is turned off.

Trip computer
Fitted to models at the top end of the range, the trip computer provides information on the following functions:

> Time of day (TIME button)
> Journey time (E/T)
> Journey distance (MILES)
> Total fuel used (GAL)
> Average fuel consumption (MPG)
> Average speed (MPH)

the 'ON' position, accelerate to the desired speed and press the 'SET' button. You can now remove your foot from the throttle. If you wish to travel faster for an overtaking manoeuvre, use the throttle in the normal way. The cruise control will return the vehicle to the set speed when you release the throttle. If you use the brakes, the cruise control will not re-engage until you move the slide switch to 'RESUME'.

To alter the set speed, simply brake or accelerate to the desired speed and press the 'SET' button again.

The cruise control memory will be erased when

To set the clock time, press the 'TIME' button and move the 'RESET' button downwards to set hours, upwards to set minutes. To zero any of the other functions, press the appropriate button and move the 'RESET' button downwards. The computer memory will now record the relevant information until it is full, when the word 'FULL' will be displayed. The required information will be displayed when the relevant button is pressed. The right-hand switch gives a choice of metric or Imperial units.

Elapsed time is not recorded when the ignition is switched off. If the battery is disconnected, the

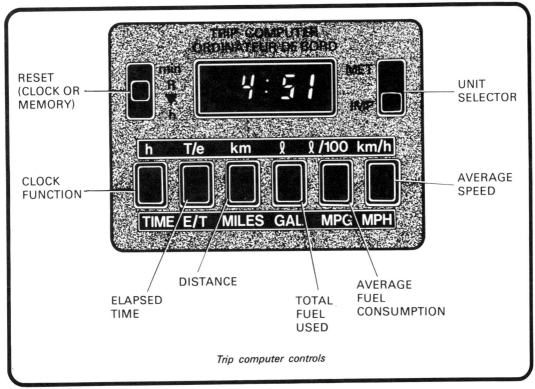

Trip computer controls

computer memory will be erased or saturated. Average speed and fuel consumption figures should not be regarded as accurate during the first few minutes of any journey.

Central door locking

On cars equipped with this facility, all passenger doors are locked or unlocked when the driver's door is operated, either with the key or from inside. Note that if the driver's door is closed with the lock button depressed, the door will remain locked — so make sure the key has been removed from the car first!

Sunroof

To open the sunroof, squeeze the bars of the locking latch together and move the roof panel to the desired position. Make sure that the latch locks the roof in position when released. Closing is accomplished in a similar fashion.

Miscellaneous

Bonnet release

The bonnet release lever is in a recess to the front

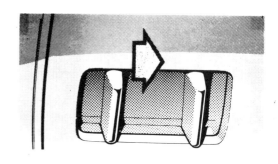

Sunroof catch. Move in direction of arrow to open

of the left-hand door. Pull the lever to release the bonnet to the first position. At the front of the car, depress the bonnet slightly and release the safety catch (see illustration). Raise the bonnet and support it on the prop.

To close the bonnet, unhook the prop and fit it into its clip. Lower the bonnet and press down firmly so that both the safety catch and the main catch engage.

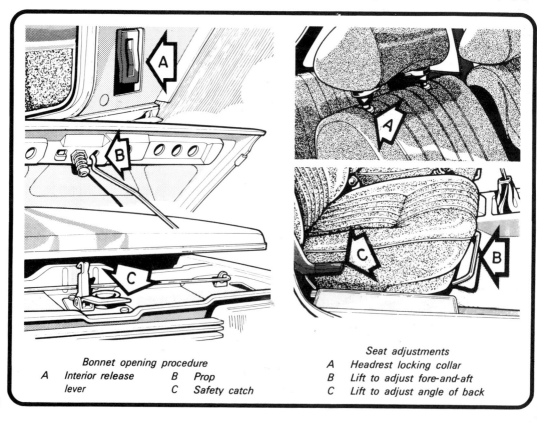

	Bonnet opening procedure			Seat adjustments	
A	Interior release lever	B	Prop	A	Headrest locking collar
		C	Safety catch	B	Lift to adjust fore-and-aft
				C	Lift to adjust angle of back

Seat adjustment

Fore-and-aft adjustment of the seats is achieved by lifting the bar at the base of the front of the seat, then sliding the seat forwards or rearwards as desired. Make sure that the catch engages positively when the bar is released.

The angle of the seat lock can be adjusted on some models by lifting the lever on the door side of the seat. Release the lever after moving the seat back to the desired position.

When headrests are fitted, they can be adjusted by rotating the locking collars round the headrest legs. The headrests can be removed by adjusting them to the highest position and then lifting them out.

Filling Station Facts

Whatever else a motorist may choose to ignore when it comes to motoring, a regular visit to a garage for the replenishment of fuel will be necessary. During such visits the wise motorist will make basic checks to ensure that the engine oil and coolant levels are correct, and also that the tyre pressures are as specified (see the *Quick-Check Chart*). These are items which can easily be overlooked, but which are nevertheless essential maintenance checks and affect the vehicle's safety and reliability.

Whilst the experienced motorist is (or should be) fully aware of these filling station check procedures, the novice may need a little guidance. It should be mentioned that these checks are particularly essential when on a long journey, especially on motorways.

As with most things, there's a right and a wrong way to go about the various filling station checks and the following points should be borne in mind when you're carrying them out...

Checking tyre pressures

Garage tyre pressure gauges are notoriously inaccurate, and it's not really surprising, the way people throw them in a heap on the floor after they've finished with them. This is somewhat disturbing since it's one of the few free services left to motorists and they even abuse that! If facilities exist to hang the line and gauge up then it's a good idea to hang them up out of the way so that the next user doesn't come along and run over the gauge. Of course it isn't always possible to check your pressures at the same garage, so it'll pay to carry a pocket tyre pressure gauge and by using this all the time you'll be certain about any pressure variations.

When checking tyre pressures don't forget to check the pressure in the spare. In the event of a puncture, one flat tyre is a bit of a 'let-down', but having two is really deflating!

Remember that tyre pressures can only be checked accurately when the tyres are cold. Any tyre that's travelled more than a mile or so will show a pressure increase of several pounds per square inch

Checking a tyre pressure

(psi) — maybe more than 5 psi after a longer run. So a certain amount of 'guestimation' comes into checking tyres if they're warm.

Since the pressures won't increase for any reason other than heat the least you can do is to ensure that the pressures in the two front tyres are equal, bearing in mind that they may be a bit above those shown in the table. (The same applies to the two back tyres, but remember that their pressure may be different from the front).

If one tyre of a pair has a low pressure when hot, bring it up to the pressure of the other at the same end of the car; if they're both below the recommended cold pressure although warm, the safest thing to do is to bring them up to about 3 psi above it, to allow for cooling.

Topping up oil

Whenever you top up the oil level, always try to use the same grade and brand; and do avoid using cheap oil — the initial saving will probably be lost in increased engine wear over a prolonged period — or perhaps a short one!

When checking the oil level, ensure that the car's standing on level ground. The engine should have been switched off for a couple of minutes at least, otherwise you may get a false low reading because of the oil still in circulation.

Open the bonnet (see *In the Driving Seat*) and find the dipstick. It's at the front of the engine. Unplug the warning light connector, if your car has that system, then pull the dipstick out and wipe it clean. (Some garages provide paper towels for this sort of thing. Some don't, so it's handy to carry a bit of rag tucked in a corner somewhere under the bonnet. Saves wiping the dipstick on your handkerchief.) Put the dipstick back in its hole — make sure it goes all the way in — then pull it out and read the oil level. If the level is approaching the 'low' mark, top up via the filler cap. You need about a litre (nearly a quart) of oil to raise the level from 'low' to 'high' on the dipstick.

When the oil level is correct, refit the dipstick securely and reconnect the warning light plug (if applicable). Don't forget to put the filler cap back on, if you had to undo it.

Even if your Alpine or Solara is fitted with the oil level warning light system, it's well worth checking the level in the traditional way from time to time, especially before a thrash up the motorway.

Checking coolant level

This is an easy check. With the bonnet open, find the radiator expansion bottle — it looks like a big jam jar and is usually located in the front left-hand area of the engine bay. The coolant level should be between the MAX and MIN marks on the side of the jar when the engine's cold, and maybe a bit higher when it's hot.

If topping up is necessary, or the bottle is so dirty that you can't see the level, you'll have to take the top off the expansion bottle. **CAUTION:** *Take care to*

Withdrawing the dipstick

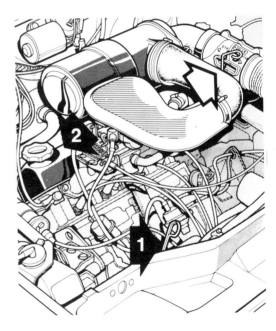

Dipstick (1) and oil filler cap (2). Third arrow points to air cleaner summer/winter adjustment lever

avoid scalding if the engine is hot. Cover the expansion bottle cap with a piece of rag and turn the cap slowly anti-clockwise to allow any steam to escape. Only remove the cap when any pressure has been released. Top up with clean water to the MAX mark on the bottle, then screw the cap back on.

Topping up should not be necessary on a regular **23**

Removing the expansion bottle cap. System should be cold

Fuel filler flap. Turn cap anti-clockwise to remove

basis with this type of cooling system. If it is, then coolant is being lost somewhere and the cause should be investigated. Remember too that if you keep adding plain water, you're diluting the antifreeze mixture in the engine, maybe to the point where it's no longer effective against freezing and corrosion. Ideally, therefore, you should top up using an anti-freeze mixture of the same type as that already in the car, but in practice it's better to top up with plain water than to run with a low coolant level.

Self-service garages

Many garages now operate on a self-service basis so that the customer's subjected to the intricacies of refuelling his or her own vehicle. Regulars to this type of establishment need no introduction to its methods

of operation and can usually be seen going through the routine at high speed like well-oiled robots. To the newcomer, the operation of the various kinds of pump can at first be confusing, but don't panic! Carefully read each instruction on the pump in turn before attempting to work it. When refuelling, insert the nozzle fully into the car's filler tube and try to regulate the fuel flow at an even rate so that it's not too fast. Most pumps now have an automatic anti flow-back valve fitted in them, when prevents any surplus petrol making a speedy exit from the filler neck all over the unsuspecting operator. On completion, don't forget to refit the petrol filler cap.

Don't try to fill the fuel tank to the brim, or you're liable to lose some fuel out of the tank breather. Stop filling when the automatic cut-off operates for the first time.

QUICK CHECK CHART

TYRE PRESSURES

Recommended pressures for cold tyres in lbf/in² (kgf/cm²)

	Front	Rear
Normal load	26 (1.8)	26 (1.8)
Full load and/or high speed	28 (1.9)	29 (2.0)

FUEL OCTANE RATING
All models

98 minimum (4-star)

FUEL TANK CAPACITY
All models

12¾ gallons (58 litres) approx

ENGINE OIL GRADE
All models

Multigrade SAE 10W/50, 15W/50, 20W/40 or 20W/50

DIPSTICK CALIBRATION
Quantity of oil required to raise level from 'low to 'high' (all models)

1.76 pints (1 litre) approx

Fuel octane star rating symbols − use the correct grade for your model

In an Emergency

Servicing tasks and intervals have fortunately become fewer over the years, and consequently what was at one time a weekly 'rebuild' has become for many an optimistic motorist the annual chore, and this only because the MOT test is coming up! Small wonder then that the occasional spot of bother or breakdown still occurs, when the specified service checks and jobs are ignored, and this fact is even boasted about by many people.

This does not of course apply to everbody. A lot of owners religiously check, service and clean their car at regular intervals. However, even the most carefully looked-after car will let you down some day. Punctures are still a common event, and although changing a wheel isn't the major operation it used to be, it's still not a pastime to be recommended, especially as it always seems to need doing on a cold wet night; and you won't feel any better with your spouse or mother-in-law looking on in scorn as you discover that the spare's flat and you've no idea how the jack works. If you're not familiar with the jack supplied with your car, get acquainted with it — because one day you're going to need to use it!

Spares and repairs kit

The tool kit supplied with the car is the minimum necessary to change a wheel, and nothing more, so should a breakdown occur, you may well be thankful for a basic tool and spare parts kit of your own. Obviously it's not practical to motor around carrying vast quantities of spare parts and a full range of mechanic's tools, but a few of the items more likely to be needed, and easily used at the roadside, can get you out of a spot of bother. Apart from a selection of tools (these are discussed in *Tools for the Job*) the sort of things you should consider carrying are:

Spark plug — correctly gapped and clean
A length of HT lead sufficient to reach from the distributor to the furthest plug

Water pump/alternator drivebelt
Distributor rotor arm
Roll of insulating tape
A torch, or extension light and lead with crocodile clips
A container of spare coolant and a hose bandage
Fuses and spare light bulbs
Breakdown warning triangle
Tow-rope
Windscreen de-icer and scraper
Hand cleaner and rags
Your Haynes Handbook and/or Owner's Workshop Manual

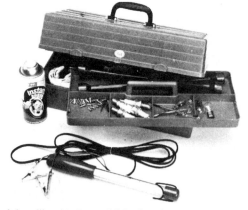

A box like this is useful for keeping your emergency repair kit together

An 'Instant Spare' aerosol in use on a flat tyre

If you want to carry emergency petrol, use an approved safety can of the type shown here. The detachable spout makes pouring easy

The list could of course be expanded indefinitely — for example, you might like to have a set of spare cooling system hoses instead of just a hose bandage. It's up to you to decide what you're likely to use in a roadside situation.

So far as the water pump/alternator drivebelt is concerned, it's worth mentioning that you can buy an emergency type which doesn't require any bolts to be loosened to fit it, and which will suit a wide variety of cars. With one of these in the car, you can get on your way quickly and fit a proper replacement belt at your leisure.

Another item well worth carrying is an aerosol can of ignition waterproofer, which is particularly beneficial on damp mornings and when motorway spray and rain get into your ignition system. If the car fails to start or misfires under these conditions, a quick squirt applied to the coil, ignition leads and distributor cap will chase off any moisture present and save much time and aggravation drying and cleaning the various individual components.

A further 'get you home' device worth carrying is an instant puncture repair in the form of an aerosol can. The nozzle is screwed on to the tyre valve, and releases sealant to seal the leak, together with gas to reinflate the tyre. It's suitable for tubed or tubeless tyres and will at the very least allow you to drive to a garage without getting your hands dirty.

Roadside breakdowns

If you break down or have to stop in an inconvenient spot such as a narrow road or just round a bend, pull over as far as possible to the left of the road and switch on your hazard warning lights. If you carry a warning triangle, place this in the road about 50 yards to the rear of your car facing the following traffic.

Where you're unable to repair the fault and have to walk for assistance, lock the car up and leave the sidelights on if dusk is falling.

If you have children or a dog with you, keep them under close control and don't let them run around and create an extra danger. Don't leave young children in an unattended car.

A breakdown on a motorway can be an alarming experience owing to the speed of other traffic. Pull the car on to the hard shoulder and switch on the hazard or sidelights. The 100-metre posts have arrows on them pointing the direction of the nearest emergency telephone which links you with the motorway police, who in turn will put you in touch with the AA or RAC if you're a member.

Return to your car as quickly as possible but keep well away from the carriageway. It may well be safer not to remain in the car while awaiting help, but in this case do get well away from the hard shoulder on to the verge or bank.

Jacking up and changing a wheel

Whenever the car's to be jacked up (either to change a wheel or for any other purpose) the car must be parked on firm, flat ground. The jack supplied with the vehicle is intended only for raising the car in the event of a puncture to change the wheel. It shouldn't be used to lift the car to perform any major tasks underneath unless it's further supported with chassis stands or blocks to make it secure.

Before jacking up, make sure the handbrake's firmly applied, engage first gear (or 'P' on automatics), and place blocks of some description each side of the wheel diagonally opposed to the one to be changed.

The jack and wheelbrace are clipped to the wing valance inside the engine compartment. The spare wheel is secured beneath the rear end of the car. To remove it, lift up the luggage compartment carpet and slacken the carrier bolt using the wheelbrace until the wheel can be withdrawn from beneath the vehicle.

Lever off the wheel trim (if fitted) and use the

Jack and wheelbrace stowed in engine compartment

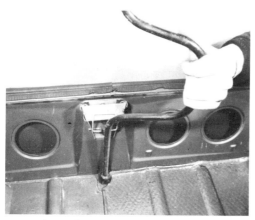

... to release the spare wheel from its cradle

Slacken the bolt with the wheelbrace...

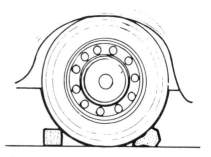

28   *Jack head engaged in jacking point*

Always wedge the wheels before jacking

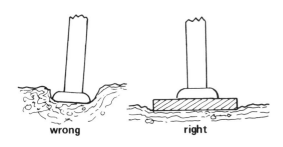

In soft ground, use a piece of wood under the foot of the jack

Locating stud (arrowed) on front wheel

Fuse box is located in engine compartment

wheelbrace to slacken each wheel bolt by about half a turn. Insert the head of the jack into the jacking point nearest the wheel in question and raise the vehicle until the wheel is clear of the ground. (If the ground is soft or muddy, try to find a piece of wood to spread the load under the foot of the jack.) Remove the wheel bolts and take off the wheel.

If you're changing a front wheel, turn the hub until the wheel locating peg is at the top, and make sure that the peg engages in one of the four small holes in the wheel. Rear wheels don't have this peg, so just line up the bolt holes – use a piece of wood to raise the wheel to the right height. Insert the bolts and lightly tighten them with the wheelbrace. Lower the car to the ground and give the wheel bolts another round of tightening – no need to jump up and down on the wheelbrace, but do them up as tight as you can with normal hand pressure. Refit the wheel trim and thump it home with your hand.

Put the flat tyre into the spare wheel cradle if you want, but don't forget to have the puncture mended at the earliest opportunity. It might be a better idea to leave the flat tyre in the luggage area, where you'll see it regularly, until it's mended. There are few things more infuriating than to suffer a puncture in a car without a serviceable spare! Either way, wind up the spare wheel cradle before you proceed, and stow the jack and wheelbrace back in the engine bay. Remember to check the pressure of the spare tyre as soon as you can, especially if it looks a bit soft, and check the tightness of the wheel bolts again after a hundred miles or so.

Electrical failures

Apart from simple bulb failure, which is dealt with later, electrical faults can be among the most difficult problems encountered by the motorist. If the complete electrical system is dead, the cause must be either the battery itself or its connections. If it's just one component or system that fails, the first place to look (after checking that a wire hasn't dropped off this item in question) is the fuse box.

The fuse box is located in the engine compartment on the right-hand wing valance. Six fuses are fitted – see *Vital Statistics* for details of which fuse does what. If you unclip the fuse box from the wing and squeeze the securing clips together, the box will open and expose the fuses. The metal track on a blown fuse will be incomplete, and the fuse itself may have a charred appearance. Hopefully you'll have some spare fuses of the correct rating. If the new fuse blows immediately, there's a short-circuit somewhere down the line – maybe caused by a wire chafing through, or maybe due to a component defect. Where **29** one fuse serves several components, you can find out which circuit the problem is in by switching on one component at a time until the new fuse blows.

In addition to the fuses in the box, there are separate in-line fuses for the radio and central door locking system (when fitted).

When renewing a fuse, always use one of the same rating. Don't be tempted to use a fuse of a higher rating, or bypass the fuse with silver foil or wire. Serious damage to components and wiring, or even fire, could result.

If after investigating the fuses and wiring, the fault still persists, you would be well advised to consult a Talbot dealer or an auto-electrician. It is all too easy to rush into a programme of expensive component substitution, and unless you know what you are doing it is also easy to spend money on the wrong things!

Maintenance of lights

Remember that a defective exterior light can be not only dangerous but also illegal. Carrying spare bulbs will enable you to replace blown ones as they occur. A failed interior lamp or panel bulb may be just a nuisance but an exterior lamp could be a life or death matter.

Headlamp bulb renewal

Open the bonnet and unplug the wiring connector from the headlamp. Release the spring clips and withdraw the bulb complete with holder. (On some halogen type bulbs it is necessary to turn the bulb holder outer ring to align the tags with the notches.) The bulb and holder are renewed as a unit.

Insert the new bulb and make sure the notches line up. Don't touch the glass of the new bulb with

Headlamp bulb securing method may be spring clip (left) or slotted ring (right)

Unplug the headlight connector

Withdraw the headlamp bulb and holder

your fingers – this is especially important with halogen bulbs – as greasy deposits will shorten the useful life of the bulb. Clean the bulb with methylated spirit if you do accidentally touch it. Refit the spring clips, or rotate the outer ring, and reconnect the wiring plug.

Headlamp beam alignment

Most models are fitted with load adjusters on the back of each headlamp reflector. These can be set to

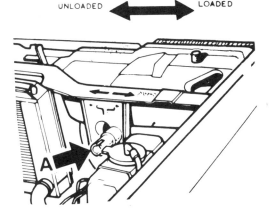

Headlamp beam load adjuster (A) – early type

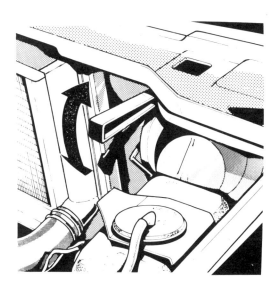

Headlamp beam load adjuster – later type

compensate for the change in vehicle attitude which occurs when a heavy load is carried in the rear. The accompanying diagram shows the operation of the adjusters.

Don't attempt any other adjustment of the headlamp beams. Special optical equipment is needed to set the aiming accurately.

Sidelamp bulb renewal

The sidelamp bulb holders are located below the headlamp bulb holders, so open the bonnet and pull the bulb and holder out of its rubber sleeve – no need to disconnect the wire. Push and twist the bulb to remove it.

Fit the new bulb and push the bulb and holder back into place.

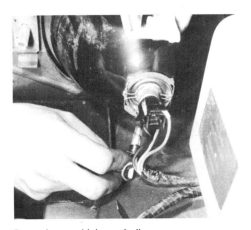

Removing a sidelamp bulb

Direction indicator bulb (front)

Undo the two screws holding the lens, remove the lens and extract the bulb. Fit the new bulb and refit the lens. Don't overtighten the securing screws or you may crack the lens.

Rear light bulbs

On early models, the appropriate lens must be removed (two or three screws) to expose the bulbs, which can then be removed. In the case of the rear number plate light, the light unit must be partially withdrawn after removing the screws to gain access to the bulb, and it may be necessary to disconnect the leads.

On later models, access to the rear bulbs is via the luggage compartment. The appropriate bulb holder can be withdrawn after releasing the catch on its back. Press the bulb holder back into place after fitting a new bulb.

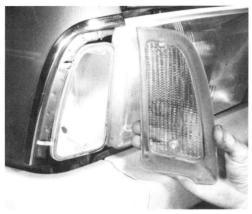

Front direction indicator bulb is accessible after removing lens

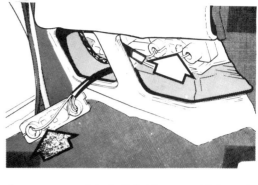

Later type rear light bulb holders are withdrawn by sliding catches (arrowed) towards centre of car

Rear light bulb access — early type

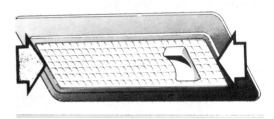

Lever off interior light cover at points arrowed

Number plate light unit — early type

Interior light bulb

Carefully lever the cover off the interior light by prising it with a screwdriver in the slot at the side. Renew the bulb and press the cover back on, being careful not to trap the wire.

Instrument panel light bulbs

The instrument illumination and warning lamps can just about be reached with the instrument panel in place. Remove the undertray, if one is fitted, and disconnect the battery earth lead — you'll be poking around in a confined space with a lot of wiring about and it would be a shame to start a fire!

Working blind, in whatever position you find least uncomfortable, reach up behind the instrument panel and locate the appropriate bulb holder. Twist and pull — carefully! — to remove the bulb and holder. Fit a new bulb to the holder (that's the easy bit), then refit the bulb holder to the instrument panel.

Like any intricate job, the above is much easier once you've done it a few times. If your hands are too big, or you haven't the patience, you'll have to take the instrument panel out, which is a job beyond the scope of this book. You'll find details in the Haynes Owner's Workshop Manual for the Alpine and Solara.

Reconnect the battery on completion, check the warning lights for correct operation and (if necessary) reset the clock.

Direction indicator flasher – renewal

If the direction indicators pack up, and you're sure that the bulbs and wiring are OK, the flasher unit may be at fault. It's located below the instrument panel, close to the steering column, and is secured by a single screw. Make a note of the wire connections before removing the old unit, or transfer the connectors to the new unit one at a time, so you don't get them mixed up.

Cable renewal

Not electrical cables, but mechanical. The items below may not qualify for emergency renewal in everyone's opinion, but it is certainly illegal not to have a working speedometer. A broken handbrake cable may inconvenience you greatly or very little, depending on where and how you drive, but again there is the legal aspect to consider. And you certainly won't get far without a throttle cable! Let's consider

the throttle cable first, as it's the only one that can actually leave you stranded at the roadside...

Throttle cable

A typical cable layout is shown in the illustration. As long as you've got a spare cable, all you have to do is to disconnect the cable at each end, unclip it and feed in the new cable. Make sure that the cable is adjusted so that the throttle plate closes completely when the pedal is released, and opens fully when the pedal is depressed – this adjustment is made at the carburettor end of the cable, by means of the clamp nut.

A more common problem is to have the cable break and no spare in sight! If the break is right at the end, there may be enough length left for you to improvise an attachment to the carburettor or throttle pedal, using a bit of soft iron wire or even string. Just make sure that your improvised method won't cause the throttle to stick open, for obvious reasons!

If the cable is totally unusable and you've no spare, you may be able to attach the choke cable to the throttle arm on the carburettor and limp to a garage like that. It doesn't necessarily have to be a Talbot garage either – many larger garages, and nearly

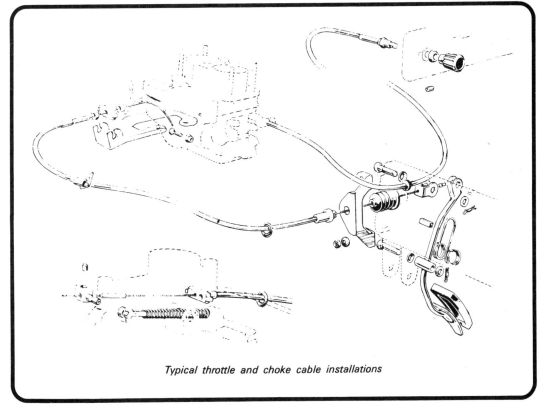

Typical throttle and choke cable installations

all motorcycle repair shops, can make up cables to the length and pattern required if you have the old one.

If your car has automatic transmission and/or cruise control fitted, you'll find a couple of extra cables are involved. The principle is the same — just take careful note of the routing and attachment of any cable before disconnecting it.

Choke cable

This is attached to the carburettor in a similar fashion to the throttle cable. At the dashboard end the choke control knob must be removed — it's held on with a grub screw — and the nuts can then be removed from the cable end fitting. Disconnect the warning light switch wires (when present) and the cable can be withdrawn.

When fitting the new cable, adjust it so that there is just a little slack when the control is pushed fully home. Don't forget to use a grommet where the cable passes through the bulkhead, otherwise you may suffer a draught and the cable may chafe on the metal.

A broken choke cable isn't quite so urgent a problem as a throttle cable. You can always open the bonnet and operate the choke lever on the carburettor by hand, whilst a helper operates the starter. Make sure the choke is completely off before you drive away, though, otherwise you'll waste a lot of petrol and maybe cause rapid engine wear as well.

Speedometer cable

You can unscrew the knurled nut behind the speedo without having to remove the instrument panel, if you're patient. It's a good idea to disconnect the battery first, especially if you want to use a pair of pliers on the nut. Push the cable through the bulkhead grommet into the engine compartment.

If you just want to renew the inner (and if you can find someone to sell you the inner alone!) there's no need for any further dismantling, provided you can get all the old inner out of the casing. With only average luck, the inner will be broken somewhere in the middle and you'll have to unbolt the cable at the gearbox end. The photo shows how it's attached. This is also necessary if you want to fit a complete new cable — often the best course, as a new inner and an old outer don't always get on together too well.

With the new cable connected at the gearbox end, feed the top end back into the car, taking care not to bend or kink the inner. Make sure the drive end has engaged properly in the speedo head before tightening the knurled nut.

If a new cable breaks after a short mileage, either there's a sharp bend or kink in it, or there may be

Speedometer cable connection (arrowed) at gearbox end

something wrong with the speedo head. Don't just keep on fitting cables in that case, it will be cheaper in the long run to get to the root of the problem.

Handbrake cable

This is definitely not a roadside job! As you may deduce from the drawing, both rear brake drums have to be removed (see *Service Scene*) in order to release the cable ends from the operating levers. After that, things are quite simple: the old cable is removed from the equaliser yoke — that's the grooved thing at the control end — and from its guides and brackets under the body.

With the new cable fitted and the brake drums back in place, the handbrake cable should be adjusted using the nuts on the equaliser yoke until the wheels are locked with the lever applied by 5 or 6 clicks. Check that the wheels are free to turn when the lever is released. It's worth greasing the cable whilst you're down there, then it may last a bit longer than the old one!

If the handbrake sticks in the 'on' position, due to corrision in the cable, you can sometimes free it temporarily by releasing the control lever, diving under the car and pulling the cable back and forth. Make sure that the car is on level ground first though, and chock a wheel to be on the safe side. The permanent cure for the problem, is, of course, a new cable.

Towing and being towed

The only way to tow something with your Alpine or Solara is with the aid of a properly fitted towing bracket. The eyes located on the front and rear bumper brackets are provided for lashing the vehicle down during transporation and are **not** designed for

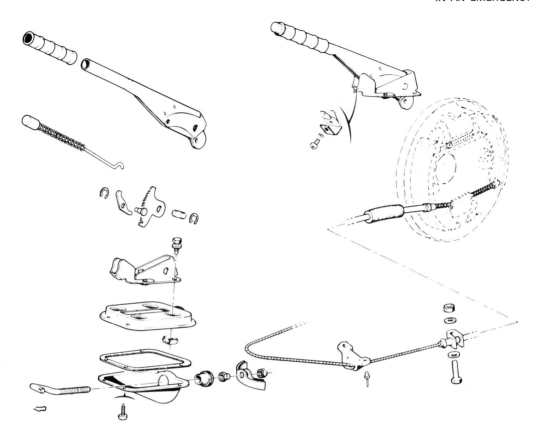

Handbrake lever and operating cable layout

towing loads. Maximum trailer weights are given in *Vital Statistics*.

If you're touring a caravan or trailer for the first time, it's well worth going somewhere quiet to practise reversing and turning round with a trailer attached — you'll soon get the hang of it, but it's better not to learn in a situation where you're holding up other traffic!

If your car needs to be towed, attach the tow-rope or chain to the front lower suspension wishbone. Make sure the rope can't foul the driveshafts or roadwheels, even on full lock. The length of the tow-rope between the two vehicles must not be more than 15 feet; don't make it too short though, or the driver

behind will be in for a nerve-racking ride! Put a sign in the rear window of the car being towed to advertise that it's on tow. Switch on the ignition (if possible) so that direction indicators and stop-lights work — or if electrical failure makes this impossible, at least remember to unlock the steering! Remember also that brake servo and power steering assistance will not be available without the engine running.

In the event of having to tow an Alpine or Solara with automatic transmission, remember to restrict the speed and distance covered (see *In the Driving Seat*). Only tow with the front wheels clear of the ground if transmission damage is suspected — this is sound advice for manual transmission models too.

Save It!

Despite the reliability of modern cars, the continuous increase in power output combined with more miles per gallon, and the greater mileages between the necessary servicing procedures, motoring costs are still relatively high. This is mainly due to high production costs and regular increases in the price of fuel. Because of this, motoring for most people has to be achieved on a fairly tight budget, and it therefore follows that running costs should be carefully analysed and wherever possible savings made. In this Chapter we cover several points which should help to reduce your daily motoring costs — or at least prevent them from increasing quite as fast as they might otherwise do, but at the same time without reducing the safety of your car.

Maintenance and driving habits

Your Alpine or Solara is potentially one of the most economical cars on the road — provided it's properly maintained! Whether you do the servicing yourself or take the car to a Talbot dealer, the aim is the same — to enable the car to run efficiently and safely. Don't skimp on servicing or postpone a major service, it's false economy.

With the engine in a good state of tune, the rest is up to you. Don't race away from every set of traffic lights, or scream up the motorway with your right foot on the floor. You'll pay for such behaviour at the petrol pump in the short term, and maybe in frequent tyre and repair bills in the longer term! This is not to say that you should drive everywhere at 40 mph, but try exercising a little restraint in your use of the throttle. You can save a lot of fuel, and avoid wear and tear, without increasing your journey times very much.

Town driving is notoriously uneconomical. Try to avoid rush hour traffic, and switch off your engine if the queue you're in looks like being stationary for half a minute or more. In lighter traffic, try to maintain a steady progress rather than alternating between full throttle and heavy braking. Remember also that the engine uses most fuel (and suffers most wear) in the first mile or so after a cold start. If your motoring consists largely of short journeys, you're never going to achieve the economy possible on the open road.

The ever-faithful roof rack has proved a boon to so many motorists, for the extra holiday luggage, but how often do you see cars being driven around with an empty roof rack still attached? Many estimates have been made of the increase of fuel consumption caused by a roof rack, due to wind resistance, and the generally accepted figure is around 10%; with a loaded rack, this figure can be as high as 30%. The moral, then, is obvious, don't use a roof rack unless you have to, and always remove it when it's not in use.

Economy devices

If we could believe everything published about economy devices, we'd be able to fit the lot and end up with a car that would save more fuel than it used! Obviously this isn't going to happen, and the evidence produced by the motoring magazines doesn't lend much weight to the various manufacturers' arguments. If you're considering fitting any of these items (which range from manifold modifiers to spark boosters and fuel pressure regulators), it can only be assumed that your car isn't giving you the miles per gallon you originally expected when you bought it. Before you lash out with your hard earned cash, first check that the engine's in good condition and that the necessary adjustments have been made correctly.

If you've recently had your engine reconditioned and are positive that it's adjusted correctly, and yet you still get poor consumption figures, it may be that the carburettor's badly worn or damaged. Your money would therefore be far better spent on having the existing carburettor checked and reconditioned by a carburettor specialist or Talbot dealer than on a dubious gadget.

The distributor and coil are likely trouble spots for poor economy. To get a complete check and diagnosis, take your car to a tuning specialist who has the necessary knowledge, and perhaps electronic diagnosis equipment, to pinpoint a trouble spot in a relatively short time, and you'll soon recover your outlay in cheaper running costs.

Smiths 'Milemiser', a useful aid to economical driving

One 'economy device' (to use the term in its widest sense) which *can* repay its cost quite quickly is a vacuum or engine performance gauge, such as the 'Milemiser' from Smiths Industries. This enables a constant check to be kept on the engine's operating range and the idea is to keep the needle in the 'good' sector as much as possible – indicating optimum efficiency and therefore minimum fuel consumption. One of these devices will quickly reveal just how important your own right foot is in the fuel economy game!

The luxurious SX versions of the Alpine and Solara are fitted with a trip computer. This useful optional extra is designed to provide the motorist with trip mileage, time and fuel consumption data. Where such a device is fitted the driver has a real advantage in being able to adjust his driving habits to suit conditions whilst obtaining the best possible fuel economy from the vehicle, but only providing it is kept in a good state of tune! The operational details of this device are given in *In the Driving Seat.*

Cruise control, as found on automatic SX models, can also be an economy aid – depending of course on the cruising speed selected! A steady speed in the high fifties or low sixties is probably the best compromise between economy and boredom on the motorway.

Fuel

Your car's designed to run on a particular grade of fuel (star rating). Don't buy fuel that's of a higher rating than this, because you're wasting your money. On the other hand, if you buy a lower rating fuel your engine performance (and probably your engine too) will suffer. If you *are* forced to buy inferior fuel, drive

carefully untill you can get the correct grade; in these circumstances it's also beneficial to retard the ignition by a couple of degrees, but you've got the bother of resetting it again later.

Lubricants and the like

Good cheap engine oils are available, but because it's so difficult to find out which cheap ones *are* good, it's safest to stay clear of them. There are plenty of good multigrade engine oils on the market and quite a few are available at sensible prices from supermarkets and the DIY motoring and accessory shops.

Unless circumstances should force you to, don't buy oil in pint or half-litre cans. This is the most expensive way of buying, particularly if it's from a filling station. The 5-litre (they used to be one gallon) cans are adequate for most purposes, and contain more than enough for an engine oil change; an extra can for topping between oil changes may be required if your pride and joy happens to be a bit of an oil burner.

Oil is also available in larger drums (which can be fitted with a tap) sometimes at an even bigger price saving. A telephone call or visit to nearby wholesalers may well prove worthwhile.

Antifreeze is always cheaper if you go to the motoring shops, but bulk buying doesn't normally apply because you never need to buy in any real quantity.

As for greases, brake fluid, etc, you'll save a little at the motoring shops but again you'll never need large quantities – just make sure that you buy something that's a good quality.

Additives

Oil and fuel additives have been with us for a long time and no doubt will be around for many years to come. It's pretty unlikely that there are any bad additives around, but there's not a great deal of evidence to suggest that there are many good ones. The major oil manufacturers will tell you that their oils are adequate on their own, in which case you'll only need additives if the oil you're using isn't much good. A fuel additive of the upper cylinder lubricant type is generally accepted as a good thing, one of its main functions being to prevent carbon building up around the piston rings and ring grooves, which means that the piston rings can seal more effectively. The way in which a car is used, whether it is just a runabout which never gets really warm or spends most of its life on long runs, has a far greater influence than additives in determining engine life.

37

Insurance

Like some of the other things that we've discussed, the service you're going to get from your insurance company will be related to the cost of the cover obtained. A cheap policy's good until you need to make a claim, and then the sort of snags you're going to come across are 'How do I get hold of an accessor to inspect the damage?', or 'How will it affect my No Claim Bonus?'

There are one or two legitimate ways of reducing the policy premium, perhaps by insuring for 'owner driver only', 'two named drivers', or an agreement to pay an agreed amount (excess) of any claim. Many large companies have a discount scheme for their employees if they use the same insurance company; this also applies to bank and Civil Service employees. You may also get a better bargain by insuring through one of the Motoring Associations if you're a member.

What it all adds up to is: (1) Insure well; (2) See what you can get in the way of discounts; and (3) Find out exactly what you're covered for.

Buying spare parts

Tyres

As you may know, Alpines and Solaras are fitted with radial ply tyres as standard equipment. Although radial tyres aren't cheap, they're definitely superior to the cross-ply tyre in both roadholding and wear potential. Don't be tempted to fit cross-ply tyres to your car as a means of saving a few pounds — the handling of the car will probably be very poor if you do fit them. When purchasing tyres, try to shop around, you've probably got a few tyre specialists in your area who give good discounts and free fitting service; and remember that your local garage or Talbot dealer may be the most expensive place to buy new tyres.

Obviously it's best to purchase one of the well known brands of tyre, but in recent years quite a few names have appeared on the scene, some of which can offer favourable price reductions. If you're considering buying tyres of a lesser known brand name, try to first acquire some independent information as to their safety and reliability.

Many suppliers give fair discounts on their tyres; some, on presentation of membership cards of certain clubs and organisations, will reduce their price even more.

In any event, tyres are expensive, and mention of their care must be made. Under-inflated tyres will cause excessive drag which will, in the short term, cause extra fuel to be consumed and if not quickly rectified will greatly accelerate their wear. Over-inflated tyres, whilst not causing so much drag, can

be dangerous and will wear to an abnormal tread pattern very quickly.

It's a good practice to inspect your tyres on a regular basis. Check the sidewalls, both inboard and outboard of the tyre for any cuts or damaged areas. Have a good look at the tread pattern and its depth; remember that a pattern that's not 1 mm deep for 75% of its area is illegal. We hope that you won't allow your tyres to wear to this extent, because not only is it illegal, it's also extremely dangerous and has been the cause of many serious accidents.

Batteries

Next to tyres, batteries are the most commonly found parts sold by the specialists. A top quality battery may cost up to three times the price of the cheapest one that'll fit your car.

Once again, price is related to the quality of the product, but isn't necessarily directly proportional. A battery with a twelve month guarantee ought to last that long and a little bit more, but batteries always seem to fail at embarrassing or inconvenient times so it's worthwhile getting something a little bit better. Many of the accessory shops and tyre dealers sell good quality batteries with two or three year guarantees. Buy one of these — it'll be worthwhile in the long run and still cost quite a bit less than the dearest ones around. And if you look after it, it'll look after you too.

By the way, before you lash out on a new battery, make sure that it's really a battery that you need — you'll feel pretty stupid if the trouble turns out to have been in the charging system!

Exhaust Systems

The average car gets through several exhaust systems in the course of its life, the actual number depending on the sort of journeys for which the car's used (lots of short journeys will mean condensation remaining inside the exhaust system and helping it to rust out more quickly).

The best place to go when your car needs a new exhaust (or maybe just part of the system) is one of the specialist 'exhaust centres' which have sprung up in recent years. They keep huge stocks to fit most mass-produced cars, and offer free fitting as well as discount prices on the parts themselves. You'll almost certainly show a worthwhile saving compared with getting your Talbot dealer to fit the exhaust (which will involve labour charges as well).

If you're planning to keep your car for several years it would certainly be worth thinking about an exhaust system made from stainless steel. It'll normally cost you considerably more than an ordinary mild steel replacement, but on the other hand should last the remainder of the car's life. If you're interested, talk it over with one of the exhaust specialists — they're usually stockists of the stainless steel ones too.

Service spares

Sooner or later the time will almost certainly come when you need a few items other than oils and grease. If you're buying on an exchange basis (eg brake shoes) please do remember to clean up the parts that you're going to exchange. Wherever possible, take along the old component for a comparison. Spare parts and accessories are available from many sources, but the following should serve as a good guide when they're required.

Officially appointed Talbot dealers: Although a Talbot garage should be able to supply just about everything for your car, it will generally be found that the prices are higher than you need to pay.

Other garages: In recent years the big British car manufacturers have introduced a replacement parts scheme whereby they market parts for each other's cars under trade names such as Mopar, Unipart and Motorcraft. You'll pay the same prices as you would from the Talbot dealer, but you may well find that your local Leyland or Ford dealer can supply you with guaranteed parts for your Talbot, and this can be a great convenience.

Accessory shops: These are usually the best places for getting your oil filters, brake shoes, spark plugs, fanbelts, lubricants, touch-up paint etc — the very things you're going to need for the general servicing of the car. They also sell general accessories and charge lower prices, but, what's equally important, they have convenient opening hours and can often be found not far from home.

Motor factors: Good factors will stock all the more important components of the engine, gearbox, suspension and braking systems, and often provide guaranteed parts on an exchange basis. They're particularly useful to the more advanced do-it-yourself motorist.

Vehicle identification numbers

When ordering spare parts (and sometimes accessories), the very least you must know is the model and year of manufacture of your car. For some items this is all you need to know, but there will soon come a time when you're asked for the engine number or vehicle identification number (which you'd always meant to make a note of but just hadn't got round to it!).

The vehicle identification plate is located either on the right-hand side of the engine compartment, or on

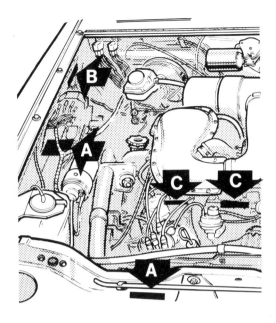

Alternative locations of identification numbers

A *Vehicle identification plate*
B *Body serial number*
C *Engine number*

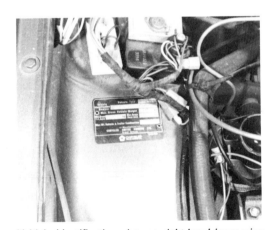

Vehicle identification plate on right-hand inner wing

the bonnet lock platform. In the latter case the plate will give a Service Number and Service Code, which may be quoted instead of the Vehicle Identification Number when ordering parts.

The body serial number is located on the right-hand wing valance.

39

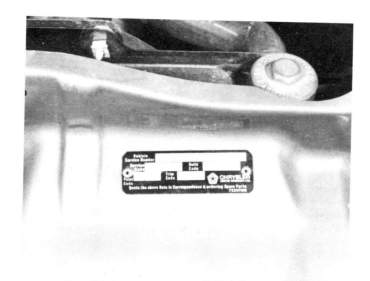

Vehicle identification plate on bonnet lock platform

The paint code is on a sticker on the left-hand wing valence.

The engine number is stamped into the engine block to the right or left of the fuel pump.

Make a note of these numbers now, in your diary or in the back of this book.

Vital Statistics

The following pages contain the more important technical specifications of the Alpine and Solara range. We're not suggesting that you need to know all these facts and figures, but you'll find it necessary to refer to this Section for the various adjustments and settings you need during the routine servicing work.

We'll start with the engine details and work our way through.

ENGINE
Type   4-stroke, 4-cylinder in-line, ohv, transversely mounted.

Bore and stroke
1.3	76.7 x 70.0 mm (3.02 x 2.76 in)
1.5	76.7 x 78.0 mm (3.02 x 3.07 in)
1.6	80.6 x 78.0 mm (3.17 x 3.07 in)

Cubic capacity
1.3 nominal	1294 cc
1.5 nominal	1442 cc
1.6 nominal	1592 cc

Compression ration
1.3 and 1.5	9.5 : 1
1.6	9.35 : 1

Firing order   1-3-4-2 (No 1 cylinder at flywheel end)

Valve clearances (cold)
Inlet	0.25 mm (0.010 in)
Exhaust	0.30 mm (0.012 in)

Lubrication system
Oil pressure at 3000 rpm, oil temperature 80°C (176°F)   3.6 to 5.6 bar (50 to 80 lbf/in^2)
Oil capacity   3.3 litres (5.8 pints) including filter

COOLING SYSTEM
Type   Pressurised, no-loss, with expansion bottle and electric cooling fan

Thermostat
Commences to open	83°C (181°F)
Fully open	96° (205°F)

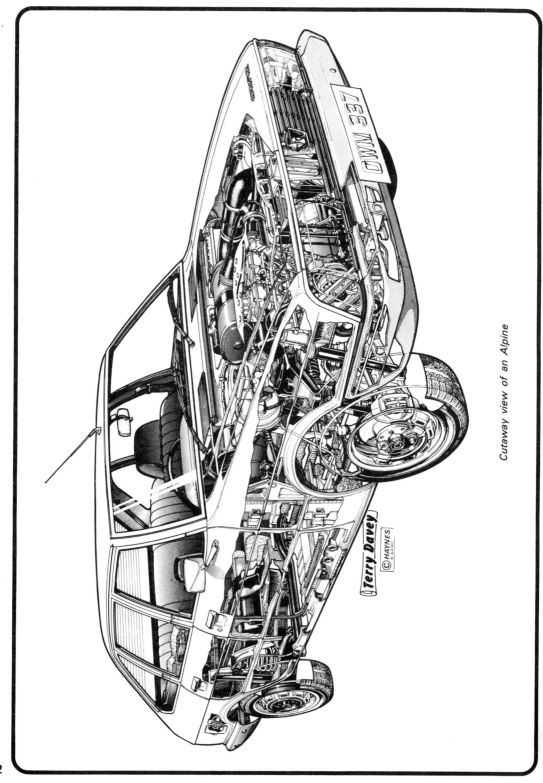

Cutaway view of an Alpine

Cooling fan thermoswitch
Switches on
Switches off

95°C (203°F)
86° (187°F)

Pump drivebelt tension

12 mm (½ in) deflection under firm thumb
pressure on the longest run

Coolant capacity

6.5 litres (11½ pints) approx

FUEL SYSTEM
Type

Rear-mounted fuel tank, mechanical fuel pump,
single or twin choke downdraught carburettor

Carburettor type
1.3 models

Single choke Solex 32 BISA, Weber 32 IBSA or
Bressel 32 IBSH

1.5 models

Twin choke Weber 36 DCNV/A or DCNV/H,
Single choke Solex 35 BISA

1.6 models

Single choke Solex 35 BISA 7, twin choke
Weber 36 DCA, Weber or Bressel 36 DCNV/A or
DCNV/H

Idle Speed
1 3 models (except engine code 6G1E)
1.3 models (engine code 6G1E)
1.5 models
1.6 models:
    Manual transmission (engine code 6J1 Eco)
    Manual transmission (other models)
    Automatic transmission

850 ± 50 rpm
650 ± 50 rpm
900 ± 50 rpm

650 to 750 rpm
900 ± 50 rpm
950 ± 50 rpm

Fuel tank capacity
All models

12¾ gallons (58 litres) approx

IGNITION SYSTEM
Type

Electronic (breakerless), distributor and coil

Distributor rotation

Clockwise viewed from above

Ignition timing*
1.3:
    Engine code G1
    Engine code 6G1
    Engine code (6G1E)
1.5:
    Engine codes Y2 and 6Y2
    Engine code 6Y1
1.6:
    Engine code 6J1 Eco
    All others

10° BTDC
8° BTDC
2° BTDC

12° BTDC
8° BTDC

4° BTDC
10° BTDC

* At idle speed, vacuum advance disconnected

VITAL STATISTICS

*Spark plugs**
Type:

1.3 up to 1979	Champion N7Y or equivalent
1.3 from 1980	Champion N79Y or equivalent
1.5 up to 1979	Champion N9Y or equivalent
1.5 from 1980	Champion N79Y or equivalent
1.6 up to 1980	Champion N79Y or equivalent
1.6 from 1981	Champion UN79Y or equivalent
Electrode gap (all models)	0.6 to 0.7 mm (0.024 to 0.028 in)

* Consult spark plug maker's literature for latest recommendations

CLUTCH
Type   Single dry plate, diaphragm spring, hydraulic
                            actuation

Adjustment   Automatic in use

MANUAL GEARBOX
Type   Four or five forward speeds, all with
                            synchromesh, and one reverse

Ratios (typical)

4-speed:	Early 1.3	Early 1.6	Later 1.3/1.6
1st	3.900	3.167	3.308
2nd	2.312	1.833	1.882
3rd	1.524	1.250	1.148
4th	1.080	0.939	1.086
Reverse	3.769	3.154	3.333

5-speed:	Early models	Later models
1st	3.167	3.308
2nd	1.833	1.882
3rd	1.250	1.280
4th	0.939	0.969
5th	0.767	0.757
Reverse	3.154	3.333

Lubricant capacity

Early models (gearbox only)	0.6 litre (1 pint) approx
Early models (final drive only)	0.5 litre (0.9 pint) approx
Later models (including final drive)	1.3 litres (2.3 pints) approx

AUTOMATIC TRANSMISSION
Type   Torqueflite A415, three forward speeds and
                            reverse

Ratios (typical)

1st	2.475
2nd	1.475
3rd	1.000
Reverse	2.103

Fluid capacity

From dry	6.4 litres (11.3 pints)
Drain and refill	3.2 litres (5.6 pints) approx

FINAL DRIVE
Type

Helical gears

Ratio
Manual transmission
Automatic transmission

Between 3.588 and 4.214, according to model
3.672 (including transfer ratio)

Lubricant capacity
Manual transmission:
    Early models
    Later models
Automatic transmission

0.5 litre (0.9 pint) approx
Integral with gearbox
1.05 litres (1.9 pints) approx

DRIVESHAFTS
Type

Three-section solid shafts comprising inner,
intermediate and stub axle sections

Joints
Inner
Outer

Constant velocity type
Universal type

BRAKING SYSTEM
Type

Discs front, drums rear. Hydraulic operation with
servo assistance. Automatic adjustment

Handbrake

Mechanical to rear wheels

Wear limits
Disc pad minimum thickness
Shoe lining minimum thickness
Disc minimum thickness after resurfacing:
    Models up to April 1980
    Later models
Drum refinishing limit

7 mm (0.28 in) including backing plate
2.5 mm (0.1 in)

10 mm (0.39 in)
11.25 mm (0.44 in)
+ 1 mm (0.04 in) on nominal diameter of
228.6 mm (9.0 in)

SUSPENSION AND STEERING
Type
Front suspension

Rear suspension

Steering

Independent double wishbone, tension bars
with anti-roll bar and telescopic shock absorbers
Independent trailing arm, coil springs with anti-
roll bar and telescopic shock absorbers
Rack-and-pinion. Power-assisted type standard
on SX and most later 1.6 models, optional on
some others

Power steering pump
Drivebelt adjustment

Fluid capacity

13 mm (0.5 in) free movement at centre of
longest run
1 litre (1.75 pints) approx

45

VITAL STATISTICS

Front wheel alignment

Toe-in (vehicle unladen)	1 to 3 mm (0.04 to 0.12 in)
Camber	0° ± 30'
Caster	2°30' ± 30'
Steering axis inclination	15°20' ± 10'

WHEELS AND TYRES

Wheel type	Pressed steel (light alloy on some models)
Tyre size	155 SR 13 or 165 SR 13
Tyre pressures	See *Quick Check Chart*

ELECTRICAL SYSTEM

Type	12 volt, negative earth
Battery	
Type	Lead acid
Capacity	40 amp hours (standard), 48 amp hours (cold climate)
Alternator	
Make	Paris-Rhone, Ducellier or Motorola
Output	35 or 40 amps (maximum)
Starter motor	
Type	Pre-engaged
Make	Ducellier, Paris-Rhone or Bosch

Light bulbs (typical)

	Wattage
Headlamps:	
Tungsten	40/45
Halogen	55/60
Sidelamps	4
Direction indicators	21
Reversing lamps	21
Rear fog lamps	21
Stop/tail lamps	21/5
Interior lamp	5
Luggage compartment lamp	4
Heater control illumination	3

Fuses

Number

6 in fuse box, plus in-line fuses for radio, central door locking and tailgate wiper (as applicable)

Application — models before 1980:

Cable/terminal	Rating*	Circuits protected
Red/yellow	16A	Heated rear window, cigarette lighter
Green/green	10A	Sidelights, tail lights, instrument panel illumination
Blue/brown	10A	Rear fog lamps
Slate/slate	10A	Heater blower motor
Slate/purple	10A	Windscreen wiper/washer, stop-lamp, reversing lamps
Red/red	10A	Direction indicators, clock, interior lamps

Application — 1980 models onwards:

Cable/terminal	Rating*	Circuits protected
Red/yellow	16A	Heated rear window
Red/red	10A	Direction indicators, clock, interior lamps, oil level warning system
Blue/brown	10A	Rear fog lamps
Green/green	10A	Sidelights, tail lights, instrument panel and control illumination
Purple/purple	16A	Heater blower motor, cigarette lighter, tailgate wiper/washer, headlamp washer
Slate/slate	10A	Windscreen wiper/washer, stop-lamps, reversing lamps

* 10A fuses are coloured green, 16A are coloured white

DIMENSIONS AND WEIGHTS
Dimensions — Alpine
Wheelbase   2.604 m (102.5 in)
Overall length:
    Early models   4.245 m (167 in)
    Later models   4.318 m (170 in)
Overall width   1.680 m (66 in)
Overall height   1.390 m (54.7 in)

Dimensions — Solara
As for Alpine except:
    Overall length   4.393 m (173 in)

Kerb weights (unladen) — Alpine
Models up to 1980:
    1.3   1050 kg (2315 lb)
    1.5   1075 kg (2370 lb)
    1.6 (automatic transmission)   1095 kg (2414 lb)
Later models:
    1.3 LE and 1.6 LE   1031 kg (2274 lb)
    1.3 LS   1047 kg (2308 lb)
    1.3 GL and 1.6 GL   1060 kg (2336 lb)
    1.6 LS   1053 kg (2321 lb)
    1.6 GLS   1063 kg (2343 lb)

Kerb weights (unladen) — Solara
1980 models:
    1.3 LS and 1.6 LS   1012 kg (2231 lb)
    1.6 GL   1024 kg (2257 lb)
    1.6 GLS   1056 kg (2328 lb)
    1.6 SX (automatic transmission)   1096 kg (2416 lb)
Later models:
    1.3 LE and 1.6 LE   999 kg (2202 lb)
    1.3 LS   1022 kg (2254 lb)
    1.3 GL and 1.6 GL   1042 kg (2297 lb)
    1.6 LS   1028 kg (2267 lb)
    1.6 GLS   1055 kg (2326 lb)

VITAL STATISTICS

Towing weights
These weights are related to the capability of the vehicle and do not necessarily reflect legislation governing trailer weights

1.3 (all models)	750 kg (1654 lb) max
1.5 (all models) and 1.6 with 4-speed transmission	900 kg (1985 lb) max
1.6 (5-speed)	1000 kg (2205 lb) max
1.6 (automatic transmission)	1100 kg (2425 lb) max

Tools for the Job

For anyone intending to tackle car servicing, a selection of good down-to-earth tools is a basic requirement. The initial outlay, even though it may appear to be something approaching the national defence budget, could well be less than the labour charges for one full service; on top of this, you should be paying less for the oil and replacement parts by getting them yourself so, provided you've two or three hours to spare, you must be on to a winner.

The tools supplied with the vehicle when new enable the owner to change a roadwheel, and that's about all. It is therefore advisable to obtain at least a basic tool kit for carrying in the vehicle in order to be able to cope with minor adjustment and possibly breakdowns. This 'basic' kit should comprise two screwdrivers (one cross-headed), a pair of pliers, a small or medium adjustable spanner, a spark plug spanner and a set of feeler gauges. A set of suitable combination spanners to cover the more common sizes should also be made up and carried. These items will be the basic essential requirements needed.

A small but important point when buying tools is the quality. You don't have to buy the very best in the shop but, on the other hand, the cheapest probably aren't much good. Have a word with the manager or proprietor if you're in doubt; he'll tell you what's good value for money.

If you intend to do the routine service and maintenance tasks on your Alpine or Solara as well, additional tools will be required. It's very difficult to tell you exactly what you're going to need, but the list below should be a help in building up a good tool kit.

Combination spanners — 10, 13, 17, 19 and 22 mm
Adjustable spanner — 9 inch
Spark plug spanner (with rubber insert)
Engineer's hammer
Spark plug gap adjustment tool
Set of feeler gauges
Screwdriver — 4 in x ¼ in dia. (plain)

Double-ended ring spanner

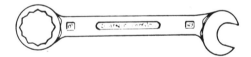

Combination ring/open-ended spanner

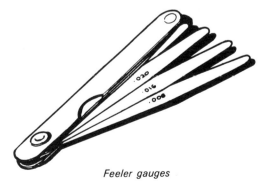

Feeler gauges

49

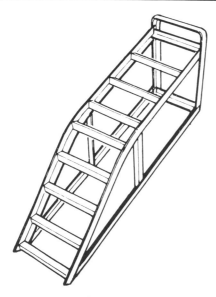

Steel ramp

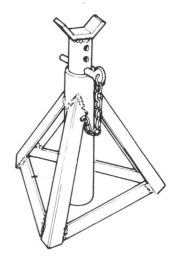

Axle stand

The Drainer Can avoids mess when changing oil

Screwdriver — 4 in blade x ¼ in dia. (crosshead)
Pliers — 6 inch
Junior hacksaw
Tyre pump
Tyre pressure gauge
Set of Allen keys (metric)
Oil can
Fine emery cloth or oilstone
Wire brush (small)
Funnel (medium size)
Hydraulic jack or strong screw type
Pair of axle stands (concrete or wooden blocks
will do if you're careful about choosing them)
Stroboscopic timing light

Additionally you'll need suitable containers to drain the engine, gearbox and axle oils into, and also one that can be used to wash parts in. An old 1 gallon oil can will do to drain the oil into if you cut a suitable size hole in the side face. An old washing-up bowl's ideal too, and can also be used to clean components in. Or you may prefer to buy a purpose-built can like that shown. Some non-fluffy rags will also be required to clean parts with and to mop-up the odd drop of oil spilt. If sawdust's available, keep some handy to soak up any major oil spillage. If you can buy, beg or borrow a boiler suit to work in, this will help to keep you clean and allows greater freedom of movement when working underneath the car.

You will find that a pair of metal ramps is a very useful investment, providing an alternative to the jack or axle stands when you want to get at the underside of the car but don't need to remove the wheel(s). Most ramps available give a lift of between 9 inches and 1 ft and you can, of course, drive either the front or back end of the car on to them — but you'll still need to engage a gear and chock the other two wheels for safety's sake.

Hopefully, your attempts at car servicing are going to show you that it can all be worthwhile, and having worked your way through the various jobs listed in the Service Schedules you'll be able to see that there are many others which can be done without becoming a mechanical wizard. For this purpose, Haynes publish a first class Owner's Workshop Manual for the Alpine and Solara models which details just about every operation that can conceivably be done on these cars. It'll mean buying a few more tools, but to hell with it — you're out to save yourself some money and get a job

done in the process.

If and when you do get to this stage, the next items to put on your tool kit shopping list are a good socket spanner set (½ inch drive, and preferably including a ratchet, extension bar, universal joint and spark plug socket) and a torque wrench for use with the sockets.

While we're talking about tools, it's worth mentioning some of the tune-up aids that are on the market. A visit to a good motor accessory shop can be an enlightening experience, just to show you the sort of things available. Later in this book, you'll find a bit about 'bolt-on goodies', but all we'll concern ourselves with here are two items.

Stroboscopic timing lamp: The only way of checking your ignition timing (that's the time at which the spark occurs) is with the engine running, and for this a stroboscopic (strobe) light is used. This is connected to No 1 spark plug lead and the beam is shone on to the timing marks. Any proprietary light is supplied with full connecting and operating instructions.

Cylinder compression gauge: This is very useful for tracing the cause of a fall-off in engine performance. It consists of a pressure gauge and non-return valve, and is simply screwed into a spark plug hole while the engine is turned over on the starter.

Two other useful items are a hydrometer, which is used for checking the specific gravity of the battery electrolyte (this will tell you if you have a dud cell which won't hold a charge), and a 12-volt lamp on an extension lead with crocodile clips which can be connected to the battery terminals.

Care of your tools

Having bought a reasonable set of tools and equipment, it's the easiest thing in the world to abuse them. After use, always wipe off any dirt and grease using a clean, dry cloth before putting them away. Never leave them lying around after they've been used. A simple rack on the garage wall, for things you don't need to carry in the car, is a good idea.

Keep all your spanners and the like in a metal box — you can wrap some rags around them to stop them rattling if you're going to carry them in the car. Any gauges and meters should be carefully put away so that they don't get damaged or rusty. Do take a little care over maintaining your tools too. Screwdriver blades, for example, inevitably lose their keen edges, and a little timely attention with a file won't go amiss.

Service Scene

This is the Chapter where you get back the money you paid for this book, and all those tools — we hope! The sight of a garage bill for a full service may be enough to make a reluctant mechanic keener, but you'll find (believe it or not) that there is actually a good deal of satisfaction to be had from servicing your car yourself, apart from any financial savings you may make.

Of course there is no substitute for experience, and you shouldn't rush into the more complicated jobs if your previous experience is limited to checking the oil! If you have a friend who's skilled in car maintenance, it might be worth getting him or her to oversee what you're doing at first, especially where safety-related items like brakes are involved. And remember, all jobs are easier after the first time.

Even if you prefer to leave servicing to the professionals, do have a look at the weekly checks at the beginning of the service schedules. The few simple items there will only take a few minutes, but they could save untold expense, or even your life, by enabling you to spot a developing fault before it gets serious. In fact you'll find as you work through the schedules that a large part of the work consists of inspecting components or checking fluid levels. Nine times out of ten your check may show nothing wrong — don't get complacent and give up checking for that reason though!

Some people may ask 'why service the car at all? If it's running all right leave it alone'. This is an attitude inviting disaster. Servicing or inspection of the vehicle's main components at regular intervals is necessary to keep the car safe, to prolong its active life, and to maintain a sensible resale value. The old maxim of prevention rather than cure was never truer than in connection with car servicing. Whether it be casting your eagle eye over the general workings of the car or getting down to the service task in a workmanlike (or workwomanlike) fashion, it's all going to be worthwhile in the long run. Remember that a worn part won't put itself right and isn't a thing to be lived with. Fix it as soon as you find it, even if it's not time for the next service.

In this Chapter, we've tried to present the servicing tasks in a logical way to minimize the amount of jacking up, etc, which may be a prelude to the actual job. The items listed are basically those recommended by the car manufacturers, but are supplemented by some additional ones which we think are well worth the extra trouble. The service

intervals themselves are something of a compromise. The modern trend is for the manufacturer to specify one all-embracing service every 10000 miles or so, with maybe just an engine oil change in between. This makes sense from the point of view of garage bills, but will involve the DIY owner in a very busy weekend! It may be better to tackle a major service in several stages, but that's for you to decide. Allow yourself plenty of time — there's nothing worse than rushing through a job on a Sunday evening in the knowledge that you've got to get the car back on its wheels for Monday morning.

If you annual mileage is very low, do at least change the engine oil every six months. This is because oil absorbs water (both from the air and as a product of combustion) which will attack the moving parts of the engine if allowed to remain in the sump indefinitely. That proverbial car which has only been driven on Sundays may not be such a bargain after all!

If you've recently bought the car, the safest thing is to go right through all the Service Schedules (not on the same day, of course!) unless you can really satisfy yourself that the previous owner was as meticulous about things as you'd like to be. You'll see that we've included Spring and Autumn check-ups, too, just so that you can make sure your car's as fit as possible for the season ahead.

Safety

Accidents do happen, but 99% of them can be prevented by taking a little care. We're going to list a few points which should reduce any accident risk, and we'd like you to read through them before starting work — it could prove to be very worthwhile.

DO wipe up grease or oil from the floor if you spill any (and you will do, sooner or later).

DO get someone to check regularly that everything's OK if you're likely to be spending some time underneath the car.

DON'T use a file or similar tool without a handle. The tang can give you a nasty gash if something goes wrong.

DO make sure when you're using a spanner, that it's the right size for the nut and that it's properly fitted before tightening or loosening.

DO brush away any drilling swarf with an old paintbrush – never your fingers.

DON'T allow battery acid or battery terminal corrosion to contact the skin or clothes. If it should happen, wash off immediately with plenty of cold running water.

DON'T rush any job – that's how mistakes are made. If you don't think you'll finish the job in time, do it tomorrow, but try not to make this an excuse for forgetting about it.

DO take care when pouring brake fluid. If it spills on the paintwork and isn't removed immediately, it'll take the paint off. And wash your hands well afterwards as it's poisonous.

DON'T run the engine in the garage with the doors closed.

DON'T work in an inspection pit with the engine running – the fumes will tend to concentrate at the lowest point.

DO keep long hair, sleeves, ties and the like well clear of any rotating parts when the engine's running.

DON'T grab hold of ignition HT leads when the engine's running – there's the possibility of a severe electric shock, particularly if the leads are dirty or wet.

DO chock the rear wheels when jacking up the front of the car and vice versa. Where possible, also apply the handbrake and engage first or reverse gear.

DON'T rely on the car jack when you're working underneath. Axle stands or wooden or concrete blocks should be used, but choose the points of support sensibly to prevent damaging anything.

DO take appropriate precautions against fire, especially when work involves disconnecting fuel system components. A fire extinguisher suitable for use on petrol and oil fires should be part of your servicing equipment.

DO seek professional medical advice if you are unfortunate enough to injure yourself.

SERVICE SCHEDULES

WEEKLY, BEFORE ANY LONG JOURNEY, OR EVERY 250 MILES

The following tools and materials will be needed, or should be available:

Lint-free rag, tyre pressure gauge, funnel, engine oil, coolant mixture, distilled water, brake hydraulic fluid

1 Check engine oil level

If your Alpine has an oil level warning system – all Solaras have anyway – you may not think you need to bother with this check. For the minimal effort involved, though, it's probably worth making sure that the warning light is telling the truth...

With the car parked on level ground, raise and support the bonnet. If the engine's been running, allow it to stand for a few minutes so that all oil can return to the sump before checking.

Unplug the wires from the dipstick (on models with an oil level warning light) and withdraw the dipstick. (Be careful of the electric dipstick, it is delicate!) Wipe it clean with a clean rag, stick it back into its hole until it's home, then withdraw it again and read the oil level. If the level is approaching the low mark (or horrors, below it) then top up with good quality multigrade engine oil – ideally the same sort as what's already in the sump, but don't run around with a low level for that reason. The oil filler cap is on the right-hand end of the engine (the car's right-hand side, not yours) and on top. Don't forget to refit the cap when you've finished, and mop up any spillage. Don't overfill either – from 'low' to 'high' on the dipstick takes about a litre (1¾ pints).

If you seem to be frequently topping up the engine oil, it could be that there's a leak somewhere, which should be obvious if it's losing much oil. The other way of losing oil is via the exhaust pipe – if the engine's burning a lot of oil you may well notice a cloud of blue smoke behind you, and there will certainly be clues on the spark plug electrodes (see the 5000-mile schedule). There's no need to panic over slow oil loss, as long as you don't let the level fall too low and can afford to keep topping up!

2 Check coolant level

You can see the coolant level in the glass expansion bottle (if it's not too dirty) without removing the cap. With the engine cold, the level must be between the MIN and MAX lines. If topping up is necessary, take care to avoid scalding if the engine is hot. Place a cloth over the expansion bottle cap and slacken it to release any steam pressure. Only remove the cap when any hissing has stopped.

Top up to the MAX mark, preferably with an antifreeze/water mixture of the same concentration as that in the system. Use plain water if you've nothing else, but remember you're reducing the antifreeze **53**

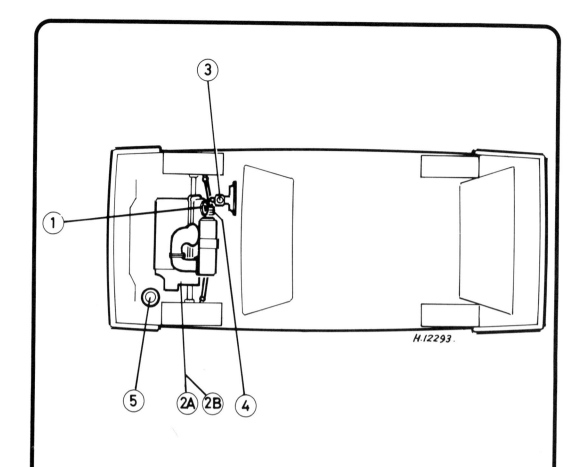

H.12293.

Lubrication chart

Component or system	Castrol product
1 Engine ...	GTX
2A Manual gearbox ...	Hypoy EP 90
2B Automatic transmission ...	TQ Dexron® II
3 Brake hydraulic reservoir ...	Universal Brake and Clutch Fluid
4 Power steering ...	TQ Dexron® II
5 Cooling system ...	Anti-freeze

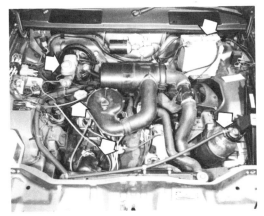

Under-bonnet check points. Arrows show (clockwise from top) battery, coolant expansion bottle, oil dipstick, oil filter and brake fluid reservoir

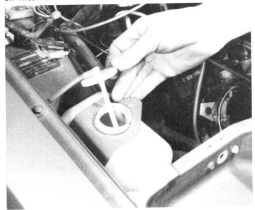

Windscreen washer reservoir

Topping up the battery with distilled water

concentration and that antifreeze also protects against corrosion. Refit the cap on completion.

As with engine oil, the need for frequent topping up points to a leak somewhere which should be located and put right sooner or later.

3 Check windscreen and tailgate washer levels

You might as well check these while you've got the water jug out. The windscreen washer reservoir is in the engine bay, the tailgate washer reservoir (if applicable) is at the left-hand side of the luggage area. Top up with water, and add a proprietary screen wash compound if you wish, but **don't** use engine antifreeze in the screen washer — it will rot the wiper blade, smear the windscreen and stain the paintwork. A little methylated spirit added to the water in winter will stop it freezing.

4 Check battery electrolyte level

Whenever the battery is to be inspected or topped up, keep any naked flame away from it and **do not** smoke when checking, as the gases given off by the battery are explosive!

In most modern batteries the electrolyte level can be seen through the transparent casing. The level markings on the casing indicate whether the battery requires topping up. On batteries with patent troughs, glass balls and so on, follow the maker's instructions.

On the latest 'maintenance-free' batteries, topping up is neither possible nor required, so you can forget this task.

If the electrolyte level has dropped, remove the covers and add distilled or de-ionized water to each cell until the separators are just covered. At the same time, the top of the battery should be wiped clean with a dry cloth, to prevent the accumulation of dust and dampness which may cause the battery to become partially discharged over a period.

5 Check brake fluid level

As with the oil level, you may well have a warning light for low brake fluid level, but that doesn't mean that you shouldn't check it yourself sometimes. The reservoir (on the engine compartment bulkhead on the right-hand side) is translucent, so you can check the level without removing the cap. The level should be between the MIN and MAX marks on the side of the reservoir.

If topping up is necessary, remove the cap (disconnect the warning light wires if so equipped) and top up using clean hydraulic fluid of good quality. The need for frequent topping up suggests a leak somewhere, which must obviously be attended to without delay. A *slow* fall in level as the pads wear is normal.

Brake fluid reservoir— early type without switch on cap

On manual gearbox models, the brake fluid reservoir also serves the clutch hydraulic system, so a fall in fluid level could be due to a leak there.

Remember to wipe up spilt brake fluid immediately — if the spillage is on the car paintwork, follow it up with lots of clean water, otherwise the brake fluid will strip the paint. And wash your hands, as it's poisonous too.

6 Inspect engine compartment

You've finished the under-bonnet checks for this week, but just have a glance around the engine bay before you close the lid. Look for signs of oil, water or fuel leaks, for loose electrical connections and chafed wires — in fact for anything that might be about to bring your car to an unwanted halt. It's useful to get to know the appearance of the engine bay when all's well so that you can spot any deviation from normal.

7 Check tyre pressures

Check all the tyre pressures with your trusty garage — see the *Quick Check Chart* for pressures. If you don't have a pump you'll have to make good any low pressures next time you go to a garage with a working air line. Suspect a slow puncture (which may not remain slow!) or a leaky valve if one tyre is always low when you check it. It's worth glancing at the tread and sidewalls too, just to make sure that no rapid wear or damage has occurred.

Really you ought to check the pressure in the spare tyre every time you check the others, but few of us are that perfect. Just try to check it once in a while, **56** or be preapred to find it flat when you need it most!

8 Check operation of all lights etc

Pressgang your spouse or innocent bystander into watching while you operate the lights, winkers, brakes etc (ignition on) and have your assistant tell you if anything's not working. Information on changing light bulbs is given *In an Emergency.*

EVERY 5000 MILES OR EVERY SIX MONTHS, WHICHEVER COMES FIRST

The following tools and materials may be needed:

Engine oil, gearbox oil or automatic transmission fluid, petroleum jelly, alternator and/or power steering pump drivebelts, set of front brake pads, spark plugs, oil drain pan, funnel, feeler gauges, Allen keys and/or sump drain plug key, spark plug spanner, wheelbrace, set of spanners and/or socket set.

1 Check Cooling fan operation

The engine needs to be warmed up for this operation, and for the next one, so maybe you should drive the car down to the local accessory shop for a gallon of oil and whatever else you need.

Open the bonnet and run the engine at a fast idle until the cooling fan cuts in — you can be getting the oil drain pan etc ready while you wait, but don't leave the car unattended with the engine running. The fan should cut in before the engine temperature gauge gets into the red zone — if not, check the wiring between the fan motor and the thermoswitch (on the left-hand side of the radiator). A defective thermoswitch can be renewed after partially draining the cooling system, or it can be temporarily bypassed so that the fan runs all the time by joining the wires together. If the fan runs all the time, even with a cold engine, either someone has bypassed your car's thermoswitch already, or the switch is stuck on.

When you're satisfied that the fan is operating correctly, switch the engine off and proceed with the next step. Remember that the fan may cut in if the ignition is switched on with a hot engine, even if the engine is not running, so *keep clear of the fan blades* when working under the bonnet with the ignition on.

2 Renew engine oil

The engine needs to be fully warmed up before you drain the oil, so that all the dirt and sludge that collects in the sump is in suspension and will drain out with the oil. The car can be on its wheels or raised at the front on ramps or axle stands — because of the angle of the engine, the oil will still drain out. You're going to have to get under the car, so maybe a piece of old carpet to lie on would be a good idea.

Find the sump drain plug — a hexagon socket-headed plug at the back of the sump — and just slacken it a quarter turn or so with your 12 mm Allen

Engine oil drain plug at back of sump

Pull off the hose ...

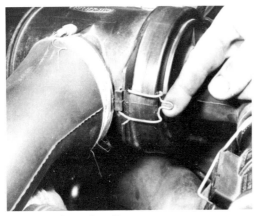

... release the spring clips ...

key or drain plug spanner. Slide your oil drain pan into position and then remove the drain plug. Try not to drop the drain plug into the pan, and remember that the oil will be hot.

Come out from under the car and put the drain plug in a safe place (or make a note to retrieve it from the drain pan). Wipe it clean. Remove the oil filler cap (on top of the engine) to assist the oil to drain freely. Let it drain for at least ten minutes — get on with something else in the meantime if you want, but don't start the engine before refilling with oil!

Remove the drain pan, wipe clean around the drain hole and refit the drain plug, tightening it securely. Fill the engine with fresh oil, using a bit less than the amount specified in *Vital Statistics* at first. Allow a couple of minutes for the oil to trickle down, then check the level on the dipstick and add a bit more if necessary, up to the high mark. Recheck the level after the engine has been run, and keep an eye on the drain plug for leaks.

When it comes to disposing of the old oil, don't just pour it down the drain — that's illegal as well as anti-social. Put it in an old oil can or some other disposable container (even a strong plastic bag, if you can seal it securely) and put it out for the dustman. Your local council will advise you of any special arrangements for collecting this sort of waste. Most garages have disposal tanks for old oil, too. Some people actually use old oil to paint the underside of the car to prevent corrosion — messy — or to mix with creosote to make a heavy-duty timber preservative. And you can also get greenhouse heaters that run on the stuff.

3 Clean air filter housing

This is an easy one. The air cleaner is that big black cylinder at the rear of the engine bag with a couple of fat rubber hoses attached. Ease off the end hose, release the spring clips and withdraw the endplate complete with filter element.

Tap or blow off any loose dirt on the filter element — don't try to clean it with solvent. Wipe clean the inside of the filter housing, being careful not to sweep dirt into the carburretor intake pipe. Renew the element if it is obviously filthy, wet, torn or oil-soaked; otherwise, just put it back (lining up the arrows on the housing and the endplate), snap on the spring clips and refit the hose.

4 Check/adjust alternator drivebelt

The alternator drivebelt also drives the water pump. A slack belt can lead to overheating and/or battery charging problems, whilst a frayed or cracked belt can make some very expensive-sounding noises **57**

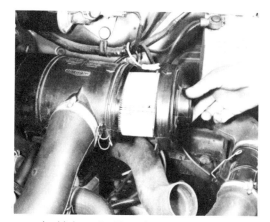

... and withdraw the filter element

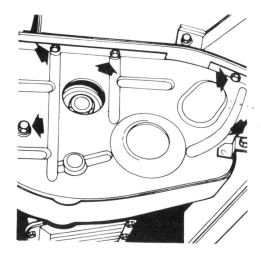

Drivebelt guard securing bolts (arrowed)

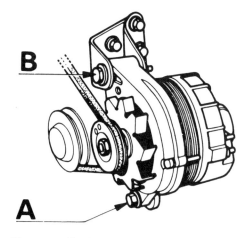

B

A

Alternator adjusting link bolt (A) and pivot bolt (B)

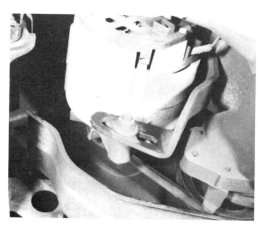

Adjusting link nut and bolt – access is easier from below

as it deteriorates. The belt may be covered by a guard (on the right-hand end of the engine) in which case you'll need to remove that first.

Check the belt tension by pressing and pulling firmly at the midpoint of the longest run of the belt. The deflection obtained should be compared with that specified (see *Vital Statistics*). If adjustment is needed, slacken the alternator pivot and adjusting link bolts – the latter is more easily reached from below – and move the alternator away from the engine to increase belt tension, towards the engine to reduce it (or to remove the belt). Tighten the link bolt when adjustment is correct, then tighten the pivot bolts. You may find it helpful to have an assistant hold the alternator in the correct position whilst you do the business with the bolts – or use a piece of wood to

lever against the alternator bracket (**not** against the body of the alternator) to achieve the desired result.

If on inspection the drivebelt is cracked or frayed, or has simply been in service for longer than you can remember, it is best renewed now. Slacken the old belt as described above until you can slip it off the pulleys, then fit and tension the new belt. A new belt may stretch quite rapidly at first, so recheck it after a few hundred miles.

From mid-1982 a smaller alternator pulley was used. That means using a shorter drivebelt too – make sure you get the right one.

5 Check power steering drivebelt and fluid level (if applicable)

The power steering pump drivebelt is adjusted in the same way as the alternator drivebelt – refer to the illustration to see the location of the pump securing bolts and the correct point to apply leverage. **Don't** use the fluid reservoir or filler neck to move the pump with, it's not strong enough.

The power steering fluid should be hot when a level check is made – if not, start the engine and turn the steering wheel from lock to lock a few times. (Don't do this more than five times without moving the car, to avoid scuffing a bald patch on the front tyres, and don't hold the steering on full lock for more than 15 seconds at a time). Switch off the engine and withdraw the dipstick from the top of the pump reservoir. Wipe the dipstick, re-insert it, withdraw it and check the fluid level. Top up if necessary with the correct grade of fluid – look for leaks if frequent topping up is needed. Refit the cap on completion.

Power steering pump drivebelt adjustment – slacken bolts (arrowed, left) and lever upwards as shown

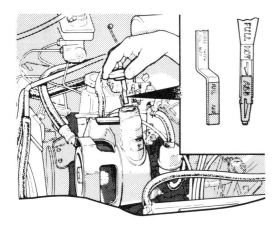

Power steering dipstick location and markings

6 Inspect spark plugs, clean and reset gap or renew

The removal and initial inspection of each spark plug can tell the owner a considerable amount about the condition of the engine. The ideal plug nose should be grey in colour with a light carbon deposit and an insulator just tinged with brown. White electrodes indicate too weak a carburettor setting and heavy oil deposits fouling the electrodes indicate surplus lubricant in the cylinder.

If you remove and deal with just one spark plug at a time, there's no danger of getting the HT leads mixed up. Otherwise, label them 1 to 4 (No 1 at the flywheel end, remember) to save a lot of head-scratching later! Remove the plug caps by pulling on the rubber boot, **not** the HT lead itself. Use a proper plug spanner, or a socket spanner and extension, to get round the problem of limited access to some of the plugs. Try to remove any dirt from around each plug before unscrewing it.

Plugs which are very dirty, or where the electrodes are obviously badly worn, are best renewed. Cleaning using an abrasive blasting machine may be satisfactory, but cleaning with petrol and a wire brush is no longer recommended. Assuming the plugs to be in serviceable condition, check the electrode gap (see *Vital Statistics*) using a feeler gauge of the correct thickness. The gauge should be a firm sliding fit. If adjustment is necessary, tap the side electrode gently to reduce the gap, or bend it carefully to increase the gap. Take care not to damage the centre electrode or its insulation when doing this.

Screw the spark plugs back into their holes by hand to avoid cross-threading, using a smear of grease on the threads to prevent them seizing up. Use the spanner for the final tightening, taking care not to overdo it – one-quarter of a turn past the point where the plug washer makes contact with its seat should be sufficient. Don't forget to refit the special cupped washers if your model has these.

Don't reconnect the HT leads yet, since they'll need to be removed for the next job...

7 Check condition of HT components

Remove the distributor cap – it's held on by two spring clips, and may be protected by a sort of rubber glove shield. Don't try to remove any leads from the **59**

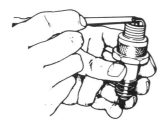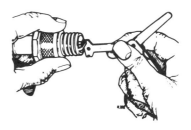

*Checking plug gap with feeler
gauges*

*Altering the plug gap. Note use
of correct tool*

Spark plug maintenance

*White deposits and damaged
porcelain insulation indicating
overheating*

*Broken porcelain insulation
due to bent central electrode*

*Electrodes burnt away due to
wrong heat value or chronic
pre-ignition (pinking)*

*Excessive black deposits
caused by over-rich mixture
or wrong heat value*

*Mild white deposits and elec-
trode burnt indicating too
weak a fuel mixture*

*Plug in sound condition with
light greyish brown deposits*

Spark plug electrode conditions

Removing a spark plug using a socket spanner and brace

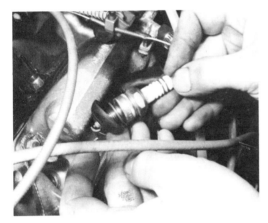

Special capped washer fits in plug recess

Removing the distributor cap. Protective shield is still in place

cap or the coil unless they are obviously damaged. Wipe clean inside and outside the distributor cap and use a fine file to clean up the metal segments inside the cap if necessary. Inspect the cap for cracks — these are likely sources of 'tracking' of HT voltage, especially in damp weather, and if present the cap should be renewed. Also clean the coil tower (the part the HT lead from the distributor cap goes into).

Carefully pull the rotor arm off the distributor and inspect its metal tip for burning. Dress the tip with a fine file if it is a bit ragged. Renew the rotor arm if it is badly burnt or cracked — it is not expensive and it is sensible to carry a spare one anyway.

Press the rotor arm back onto the distributor shaft — it will only fit one way — then refit the cap, securing it with the spring clips. Refit the shield, if one was found at dismantling, and reconnect the HT leads to the spark plugs.

8 Lubricate controls, clean battery terminals

Just a few odd jobs around the engine bay. Put a spot of light machine oil — or clean engine oil will do — onto the moving parts of the throttle and choke linkages, the bonnet catch and hinges, and any other cables and controls that catch your eye (eg the cruise control or automatic transmission cables).

Remove the battery cables — negative (earth) first — and put a smear of petroleum jelly or proprietary anti-corrosion compound (**not** ordinary grease) on the battery posts and the cable clamps. If this job has been neglected and there's a lot of 'fungus' growing on the posts, this can be removed using a solution of sodium bicarbonate (baking soda) and an old toothbrush. Don't let any of this solution get into the battery, though — when you see how it makes the 'fungus' fizz you'll understand why — and remember that the deposits are acid-based, so keep them off clothes, skin and paintwork. Reconnect the battery cables when you've finished, and reset the clock if you've got one.

9 Check transmission oil level

The procedure for this job varies according to whether your Alpine or Solara has manual or automatic transmission — and there are two types of manual transmission, just to make things difficult. In all cases, though, the car should be parked on level ground. Let's take it from there . . .

Manual transmission without dipstick

Bad luck, you're going to have to get under the car again. Take your 12 mm Allen key, the oil drain pan (preferably empty), a torch and maybe a squeezy bottle of gearbox oil. Look at the illustration before you go under so that you can identify the filler/level **61**

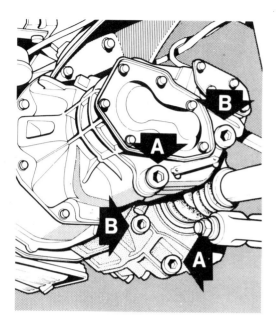

5-speed gearbox dipstick (arrowed)

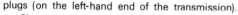

*Manual transmission filler/level plugs (B) and drain
plugs (A) – type without dipstick*

plugs (on the left-hand end of the transmission).

Clean the area around the filler/level plugs, then remove them. Some oil may drip out, so have the drain pan ready. Put the plugs down where they won't get dirty or lost, and check that oil is just up to the bottom edge of each filler/level hole. Have a care if using your finger to do this, it's easy to get stuck! Top up the oil level(s) if necessary, using the squeezy bottle, and allow any excess to drip out before refitting and tightening the plugs.

Manual transmission with dipstick

What a good idea, you can check the oil level in the gearbox in the same way as you do the engine oil. The dipstick is right at the back on the left-hand side. It's a bit hard to find, no doubt to discourage you from checking the level too often.

Having found the dipstick, pull it out and wipe it, stick it home and pull it out again. Read the level – if topping up is needed, find the breather/filler plug and undo it (14 mm spanner) and squirt some gearbox oil in there. Give it a few minutes to trickle down before checking the level again – maybe that breather could do with cleaning while you wait. Make sure the dipstick and filler/breather plug are securely home when you've finished, and mop up any spilt oil.

Automatic transmission

62   All automatic transmission models have a dipstick,

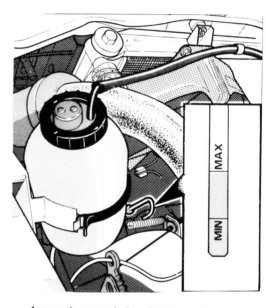

*Automatic transmission dipstick location and
markings. Later models have 'hot' and 'cold' cut-outs
to indicate correct level*

lurking by the coolant expansion bottle. There's a definite procedure for getting a sensible level reading. The engine must be idling and the transmission in position 'N', and the transmission fluid temperature must be at least 20° C (68° F). It's better if the fluid is really hot though.

With the engine running and handbrake applied,

move the selector lever through all the positions at least once, finishing up in 'N'. Wipe away all dirt from the area around the top of the dipstick, then pull out the dipstick, wipe it with a clean lint-free rag, re-insert it and withdraw it again. Now you can read the level. With the fluid cold (20° C/68° F) the correct level is near the 'MIN' mark; with hot fluid (80° C/176° F) the level should be at or near the 'MAX' mark. Top up via the dipstick tube if necessary, using only clean ATF of the specified type. Do not overfill. Make sure the dipstick is pushed fully home when you've finished.

There is a separate level plug for checking the final drive fluid level (see illustration). Top up with ATF to the bottom of the plug hole if necessary.

Driveshaft inboard gaiter (in foreground) – steering rack gaiter is visible at bottom left

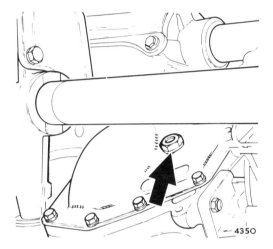

Final drive filler/level plug (arrowed) – automatic transmission

10 Inspect driveshaft and steering rack gaiters

Under the car again – you may reckon you've inspected enough down here, but it's worth checking that the driveshaft and steering rack gaiters are OK. There are two bellows-type gaiters on each driveshaft, one inboard and one outboard, and one gaiter at each end of the steering rack. If any of these are split or otherwise damaged, loss of lubricant followed by rapid wear will be the consequence. Have your Talbot dealer replace a damaged gaiter without delay, or get hold of the Haynes manual for the Alpine/Solara and see what's involved in changing the boot yourself. A new driveshaft is more expensive than a new rubber gaiter!

Whilst you're under the front of the car, you can do the first part of the next check...

11 Inspect brake pipes and flexible hoses

The illustration shows the arrangement of the brake pipes and hoses for LHD cars – RHD cars are more or less a mirror image of this set-up. The metal pipes should be checked for serious rusting or other corrosion, and the flexible hoses must be free of cracks, splits or bulges. If you find any item in dubious condition – or worse, actually leaking – get it fixed by your Talbot dealer without delay. These items are vital for safety. Don't try to fix them yourself unless you know what you're doing.

Still more inspection follows...

12 Inspect shock absorbers and mountings

There are four telescopic shock absorbers (dampers), one for each wheel. Each one should be free of leakage, and the rubber mountings at top and bottom should be in good condition. (The top mountings are visible from within the bonnet at the front, and from behind the back seat at the rear).

Renewing defective shock absorbers is quite straightforward – no repair is possible. With the car resting on its wheels, the top and bottom mountings are undone and the shock absorber withdrawn. Take careful note of the fitting sequence of washers, spacers and bushes if you decide to do this job yourself, and remember that to retain safe handling characteristics, shock absorbers should be renewed in pairs (2 front or 2 rear) even if only one is defective.

13 Inspect brake pads for wear

Even on models with a brake pad wear warning light, it's worth inspecting the brake pads while you're doing all these other tasks. That way you can decide to do the job of renewal when it suits you, rather than **63**

Brake pipe and hose routing – LHD shown, RHD similar

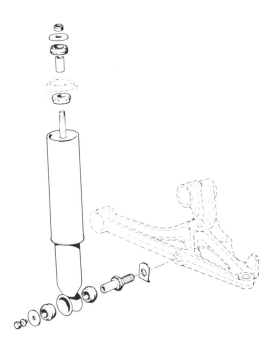

Front shock absorber and mountings

bores to accommodate the increased thickness. Use a flat piece of wood to do this, or at least something that won't damage the disc or the piston. Keep an eye on the fluid level in the master cylinder reservoir, as this will rise as the pistons are pushed back. It may be necessary to syphon a little fluid out (using a pipette or a clean battery hydrometer – **not** by mouth) to prevent the reservoir overflowing. Fit the outboard pad first, then the inboard. Make sure that the slot in the outboard pad engages with the tongue in the caliper. Slide the top retaining pin through the holes in the

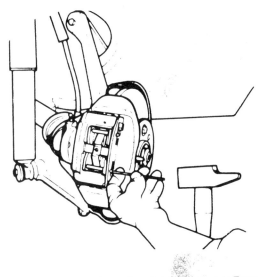

Driving out the brake pad retaining pins – early Teves type

at the whim of the warning light!

Jack up and support the front of the car and remove the front wheels. Now the calipers are clearly visible. Wipe away as much muck and crud as you can and shine your torch into the front of the caliper so that you can see the pads, one on each side of the disc. You should be able to distinguish the metal backing plate from the 'meat' of the friction material. If the thickness seems to be approaching the minimum allowed (see *Vital Statistics*), or if you're not sure about what you can see, the pads will have to come out for inspection and maybe renewal.

Start by disconnecting the pad warning light wire, if fitted, and removing its spring clip. Thereafter there are three possible procedures, depending on your car's vintage and country of origin. Sort yourself out using one of the sets of information below:

Teves (ATE) calipers up to April 1980

Tap out the two pad retaining pins from the caliper and remove the spring. Pull out the inboard pad, then gently tap the inside face of the caliper until it moves over far enough (about $^5/_{16}$ in/5 mm) for you to withdraw the outboard pad. Don't let anyone press the brake pedal from now on, or you could be in trouble.

Assuming that you're going to fit new pads, the caliper pistons will have to be pressed back into their

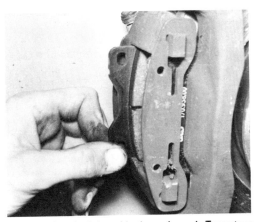

Withdrawing the inboard brake pad – early Teves type **65**

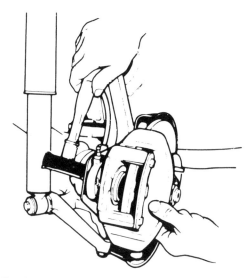

Tapping the caliper over to remove the outboard pad – early Teves type

Removing the outboard brake pad – early Teves type

by tying it up with string rather than letting it hang on the hose. Don't let anyone press the brake pedal, either. Remove the outboard pad from the fixed support.

If new pads are being fitted, press the piston into its cylinder, noting the remarks above about watching the brake fluid level in the reservoir. Fit the new outboard pad to the fixed support and the new inboard pad to the piston, then reassemble the caliper. You're supposed to use thread locking compound on the threads of the socket-headed bolts – that's why they came undone with a cracking noise. Check that the caliper moves freely on the fixed support, then put the bolt caps back and reconnect the warning light lead. Finally refit the retaining spring

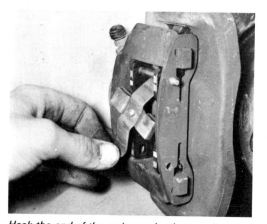

Hook the end of the spring under the top pin

caliper and pads, hook the end of the spring under it, press the other end of the spring down and slide in the other retaining pin. (If the pins don't slide but need to be brutally driven into place, maybe they need cleaning up with a little abrasive paper.)

Teves (ATE) calipers from May 1980

Remove the retaining spring from the outboard side of the caliper, then from the other side remove the two caps and undo and withdraw the socket-headed screws. The caliper can now be lifted away complete with inboard pad, taking care not to strain the hydraulic hose – support the caliper on a stand or

Removing the retaining spring – later Teves type

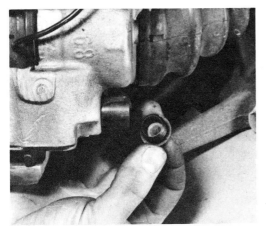
Remove the sealing caps ...

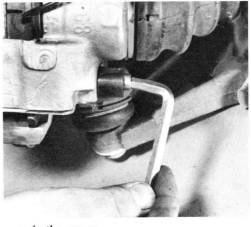
... undo the screws ...

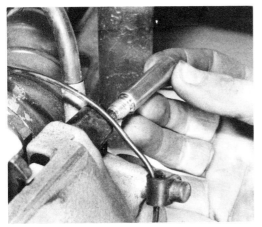
... and remove them

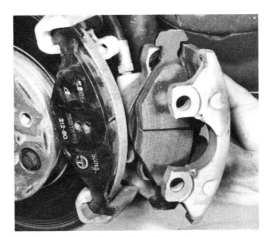
Removing the caliper – later Teves type

Removing the inboard brake pad – later Teves type

Removing the outboard brake pad – later Teves type

67

— look at the caliper on the other wheel if you're not sure how it goes on.

Bendix (DBA) calipers from May 1980

Pull out the 'hairpin' spring clip from the lower socket-headed bolt and remove the bolt. Swivel the caliper clear of the lower pin, then withdraw it downwards and support it so that the hose is not strained.

Remove the upper socket-headed bolt, then withdraw the disc pads and springs. Depress the

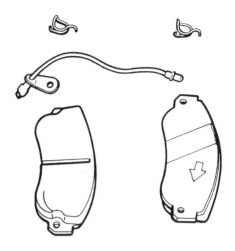

Bendix pads, springs and warning light wire. Arrow on inboard pad must point in direction of forward disc rotation

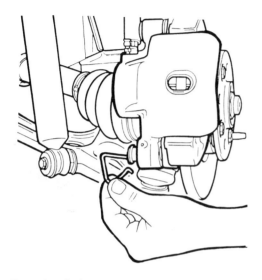

Removing the 'hairpin' spring clip — Bendix caliper

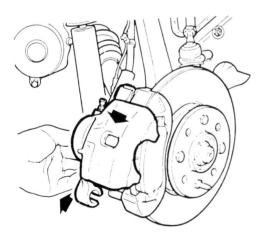

Swivel the caliper upwards, then withdraw it downwards

caliper piston if new pads are being fitted, taking precautions to avoid overflow of hydraulic fluid from the reservoir before doing so. Clean up the support pins and sliding surfaces, applying a little disc brake lubricant if possible.

When fitting the new pads, note that the inboard pad has a wide groove and an arrow which should point in the direction of forward rotation of the disc. Fit the pads and springs, then screw in the upper bolt and slide the caliper into it. Swivel the caliper over the lower pin and screw in the lower bolt. Make sure that the bolts are tight and that the caliper is free to slide on the fixed support, then snap in the 'hairpin' spring and reconnect the warning light lead.

All calipers

Repeat the operations on the other wheel — brake pads must only be renewed in complete axle sets, otherwise uneven braking may occur. When you've finished, press the brake pedal several times to bring the pads into contact with the discs. **This is important** — if you forget this step you'll be on for a nasty surprise when you try to stop at the end of your drive! Check the level of brake fluid in the master cylinder reservoir and top it up if necessary.

If you found that the old pads were contaminated with oil, grease or hydraulic fluid, or if the disc was badly scored, further repair work will be necessary without delay. This is a job for your Talbot garage or for the more advanced mechanic using the Haynes Owner's Workshop Manual.

You've almost finished this service now. Put the

front wheels back on and lower the car to the ground, then proceed to ...

14 Check tightness of wheel bolts

Do your stuff on the front wheel bolts when the wheels are back on the ground (and back on the car), then check the rear wheel bolts. (It might be an idea to slacken each rear wheel bolt slightly and then retighten it, just to make sure you can undo the bolts next time you have a puncture.)

Just a little bodywork attention now, then you can check the quality of your work . . .

15 Clear body drain holes, lubricate hinges etc

Probe the drain holes in the bottom of the doors with a piece of stiff wire to make sure that they haven't become blocked. If your car has a factory-fitted sunroof, there is a drain tube in each front wheel arch which must also be checked for blockage, especially if undersealing or painting has subsequently been carried out in that area.

Open all the doors and work your way round the car with your oil can, applying a spot to each hinge, lock and striker. Wipe off the excess when you've finished, to avoid complaints of passengers oiling their clothes! Oil the hinges of the fuel filler flap too.

Ideally you should wash the car at the end of all this, especially if there are oily fingermarks all over the paintwork, but that's up to you — it's not part of the official service schedule!

16 Road Test

Just a quick run round the block will do. Check all the gauges and warning lights for correct operation, and try the brakes to see that they work efficiently and without pulling to one side. Remember that new brake pads will take a few hundred miles to bed in before they give their best results, and try to avoid heavy braking during this period.

Have a quick look under the bonnet before you put the car away. Check the engine oil and top it up if necessary, and glance at the other fluid levels. Check the sump drain plug for leaks.

With everything in order, you've completed the 'short' service. It wasn't that short? Wait until you see the next one . . .

EVERY 10 000 MILES OR EVERY YEAR, WHICHEVER COMES FIRST

In addition to, or instead of, the work specified in the previous schedule
The following additional tools and materials may be needed:

Oil filter, strap wrench, stroboscopic timing light, 4 mm open-ended spanner, valve cover gasket, large hose clips, fuel pump sealing ring, brake shoes.

If you're starting work on a cold engine, do the valve clearances (item 2) first, since they must be done with the engine cold. Then carry on until you have to go and buy something — it always happens! — and drain the oil when the engine's warmed up. If you're starting work on a hot engine, drain the oil first and leave the valve clearance check until things have cooled down a bit.

1 Renew engine oil filter

The oil filter should be renewed at alternate oil changes, since it gradually gets clogged up with impurities and foreign matter carried by the oil. It is located at the rear of the engine, on the right-hand side, and is impossible to reach from above. You may think it's impossible to reach from below too, but it can be done.

You must have a strap wrench or chain wrench for this job — they're not expensive. Slip the strap over the filter in such a direction that it will tighten its grip as you unscrew the filter. Once you've got the filter moving, it should be possible to finish unscrewing it by hand. Remember that the filter is full of oil — about a sleeve-full — so have your drain pan handy to avoid messy spillage.

Wipe clean the filter mounting on the engine, and make sure that the old sealing ring came away with the filter. Smear the sealing ring of the new filter with a little grease or clean engine oil and screw it into position. Tighten it, by hand only, a maximum of three-quarters of a turn beyond the point where the

Oil filter viewed from below

sealing ring contacts the mounting (or as directed by the filter manufacturer). Overtightening, especially using a strap wrench, can cause real problems next time you have to renew the filter.

Check for leaks after you've refilled the engine with oil and started it up. Remember that the new filter will absorb about half a pint of oil, so allow for this in the amount of oil you use for refilling. Try a little further tightening if a small leak appears at the filter mounting. A big leak probably means that there's a problem with the sealing ring.

2 Check/adjust valve clearances

The preliminary work here is probably more time-consuming than the actual adjustment! First you've got to remove the hot and cold air intake hoses, and the air cleaner adaptor from the top of the carburettor. If the hoses are secured by those awful 'sardine-can' type clips, it's advisable to have some decent worm drive clips available as replacements. You'll also have to disconnect the little breather hose at the flame top.

Release the two nuts and one bolt holding the hot air shroud in position – that's the bit of tinware over the exhaust manifold. Undo the five remaining nuts which hold the valve cover in place and manoeuvre the cover free. If you're lucky you won't have to disconnect the throttle cable.

The valvegear is now exposed, but you've still got to devise some means of turning the engine. Remove the spark plugs – necessary anyway at some stage during this service – and jack up and support one front corner of the car so that the wheel is clear of the ground. With top gear engaged, you can turn the engine by turning the wheel. Watch the movement of the valves as an assistant turns the wheel for you –

you'll see that they move in pairs, so that as one exhaust valve is closing (rocker moving upwards), the corresponding inlet valve is opening (moving downwards). A pair of valves in this condition is said to be 'rocking'. Using the table below, you can work out which valves to adjust when a given pair is rocking. Counting from the flywheel end of the engine, inlet valves are Nos 1, 3, 6 and 8, and exhaust valves are Nos 2, 4, 5, and 7.

Valves rocking	Adjust valves
1 and 2	7 (ex) and 8 (in)
3 and 4	5 (ex) and 6 (in)
5 and 6	3 (in) and 4 (ex)
7 and 8	1 (in) and 2 (ex)

Insert a feeler gauge of the correct thickness between the valve stem and the rocker arm of the valve being checked. (Correct clearances are given in *Vital Statistics*. Remember that inlet and exhaust clearances are different.) The feeler gauge should be a firm sliding fit. If there is perceptible play (felt by vertical movement of the rocker arm being possible with the feeler blade in place) or, worse, the clearance is too small to admit the blade, adjustment is necessary. Slacken the adjusted locknut (12 mm) and use a 4 mm open-ended spanner, or *in extremis* a pair of pliers, to turn the adjusting screw. Turn clockwise to reduce the gap, anti-clockwise to increase it, checking with the feeling blade all the time.

When the gap is correct, hold the adjusting screw from moving while you tighten the locknut – this is tricky, but gets easier with practice. Recheck the gap – it's all too easy to move the adjusting screw accidentally when the locknut is tightened, which will

Removing the air cleaner adaptor from the top of the carburettor

Checking a valve clearance

give you too small a gap. Take the trouble to get it right. Too large a clearance and the engine will be noisy and inefficient, too small and there's a danger of burnt valves.

Having successfully adjusted one pair of valves, turn the engine until another pair is rocking and adjust two more, and so on until they're all done. Then go round the cycle once more, making a final check. Fit a new gasket to the valve cover, smearing it with grease, and make sure that all traces of the old gasket are removed. Wriggle the valve cover back into position, and make sure that the gasket is properly positioned before tightening the valve cover nuts. Refit the hot air shroud when doing this. You may as well leave the rest of the plumbing off for the moment, it'll give you a bit more room for the next tasks, but lower the car to the ground before proceeding.

3 Renew spark plugs

Don't use a set of plugs for more than 10 000 miles even if they look OK – it's false economy. Check the electrode gaps on new plugs before fitting them.

4 Clean fuel pump filter

The fuel pump is on the front of the engine, on the left-hand side. To clean the filter gauze you'll need to remove the screw(s) holding the top cover on – a short screwdriver may be useful here – and remove the cover. Try not to damage the rubber sealing ring, and fit a new one if you do.

Lift out the filter gauze and clean it in paraffin or petrol. An old toothbrush is useful for this. Shake the filter dry and put it back, then refit the sealing ring and cover. Don't overtighten the screw(s). Check the pump for leakage next time you start the engine.

On early models of the Alpine it was recommended that the carburettor filter gauze be cleaned at this mileage too. This filter is easy enough to get at on Solex carburettors – it's just behind the fuel pipe union – but on Weber carbs it's necessary to take the float chamber cover off to get at it. This is probably more trouble than it's worth. If the fuel pump filter and the in-line filter (see next schedule) are properly maintained, you should be able to ignore the carburettor filter.

5 Check ignition timing

Strictly speaking you ought to reconnect all those air hoses to the carburettor now (not forgetting the breather hose). Before you do so, however, just make sure that you can find the ignition timing marks. They're visible through a rectangular hole in the gearbox bellhousing, a bit to the left of the fuel pump.

Fuel pump – remove screws (arrowed) to take off cover

Found the hole? Right, refit the hoses, get the engine into a state where it will run (full of oil, HT leads connected etc) and then we'll proceed.

You must have a stroboscopic timing light (strobe) to cope with the electronic ignition fitted to your Alpine or Solara. The cheap ones just connect between No 1 spark plug lead and the No 1 plug – they're not very bright so you may have to shade the under-bonnet area if the day is bright. More expensive lights require an independent power supply, either from the car battery or from mains electricity. Connect these up in accordance with their makers' instructions. These lights give much better illumination.

With the strobe connected to No 1 spark plug lead (flywheel end, remember) disconnect the vacuum hose that runs between the carburettor and the distributor. It should just pull off. Make sure the strobe leads are clear of any moving parts, then start the engine and allow it to idle. Shine the strobe through the timing mark aperture. You should see the mark on the flywheel apparently stationary against one of the graduations on the edge of the hole. If you're lucky it'll be the correct mark for your model (see *Vital Statistics*). If you have trouble even seeing the marks, stop the engine, turn it until the flywheel mark is visible (as you did when checking the valve clearances) and highlight the appropriate marks with quick-drying white paint. Typists's correcting fluid is ideal. Restart the engine and try again.

If you decide that adjustment is necessary – unlikely with this type of ignition – stop the engine, slacken the distributor clamp bolt (at the base of the distributor) and rotate the distributor body **slightly** – clockwise to retard the ignition (reduce degrees BTDC), anti-clockwise to advance it (increase degrees **71**

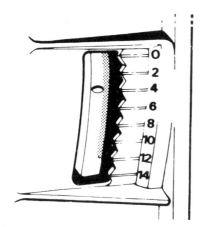

Timing aperture in bellhousing – position shown is 4° BTDC

Slacken distributor clamp bolt (arrowed) to adjust timing. Distributor cap has been removed for clarity

BTDC). Tighten the clamp bolt, start the engine and recheck the timing. Reconnect the vacuum hose when it's correct.

In the event that you don't want to buy a strobe or aren't sure about the timing marks, your local garage should be able to check the timing for you in a matter of minutes. However you do it, it's essential that the timing is spot-on before the next item is contemplated...

6 Check carburettor idle adjustment

Before you lay a screwdriver on the carburettor, a few words of caution. It shouldn't be necessary to make much adjustment to any of the carburettor settings if the rest of the engine and the ignition system are properly maintained. There's certainly no

point in trying to adjust the carb until the valve clearances have been checked, along with the ignition timing and spark plugs. Unless you have good grounds for believing the mixture to be incorrect, stick to checking and adjusting the idle speed; and don't move any 'tamperproof' devices if the car's still under warranty, or where their removal is forbidden by law.

So much for the warnings. What are you going to need? Ideally, an accurate tachometer and (if you want to check the idle mixture) a proprietary device such as Gunsons 'Colortune' to show you when the mixture is correct. Tuning 'by ear' is not recommended.

Refer to the illustration to discover the locations of the adjusting screws on your particular carburettor. It is quite likely that some or all of the adjusters will have been 'tamperproofed', either making adjustment impossible or limiting the range of adjustment. *You are advised not to remove any tamperproof devices –* if you do, make sure that you are not breaking any anti-pollution laws currently in force.

Connect the tachometer to the engine in accordance with its maker's instructions. Start the engine and allow it to idle. Adjust the idle speed, if necessary, by turning the idle speed adjustment screw. When the specified speed is obtained (see

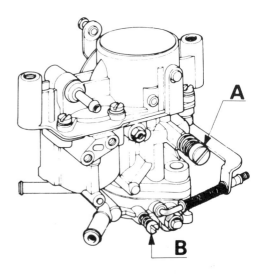

Solex carburettor adjustment screws

A   *Idle speed screw*
B   *Idle mixture screw*

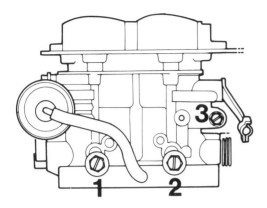

Weber carburettor adjustment screws

1 *Idle mixture, left-hand barrel*
2 *Idle mixture, right-hand barrel*
3 *Idle speed screw*

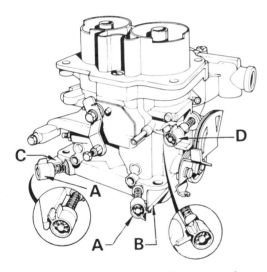

Later type Weber carburettor with tamperproof caps

A *Mixture adjustment screws*
B *Stop plate*
C *Stop plate*
D *Idle speed screw*

Vital Statistics), if the engine is idling smoothly, no further adjustment is required. If the idle is lumpy or irregular, or the engine 'hunts' (speed rises and falls), adjust the mixture as follows.

If using a proprietary mixture checking device, follow the maker's instructions. If you've nothing but

your screwdriver, the best bet is to turn the mixture control screw(s) to obtain the highest possible idle speed consistent with even running. (It may be necessary to use the idle speed adjustment screw to bring the idle speed back to the specified level.) Make adjustment by small amounts (and equally, in the case of twin choke carburettors) and note the initial position of the screw(s) so that you can return to the original setting if all else fails!

It's a good idea to have new tamperproof caps fitted when adjustment is correct, especially if you're taking the car abroad to a country with stricter anti-pollution regulations than the UK.

7 Check brake pressure regulating valve

Most models are equipped with a brake pressure regulating valve, mounted on the rear crossmember. Its function is to regulate the hydraulic pressure to the rear brakes according to vehicle load and braking effort. Check that the valve operating arm is free to move and that the spring is secure, and lubricate the operating arm pivot with engine oil.

Do not attempt to adjust the brake pressure regulating valve — consult your Talbot dealer if you suspect that it is malfunctioning, or if leakage is evident.

8 Inspect brake shoes for wear

Inspecting the brake shoes is easy enough. Some models have an inspection plug in each rear brake backplate. With the plug removed, and with the aid of a good torch, you should be able to see a small portion of one brake shoe. If you can satisfy yourself that there's more than the minimum allowable lining thickness on the shoe (see *Vital Statistics*) then that's

Brake pressue regulating valve

the end of the inspection — as far as it goes. It's preferable, though, to actually remove the brake drums and have a proper look. You'll have to do this anyway if your car hasn't got the inspection holes in the backplate, or if you have any reason to suspect wear or damage in the rear brakes.

Slacken the bolts on the rear wheel in question, chock the front wheels and raise and securely support the rear of the car. Remove the wheel and release the handbrake. One or two bolts or screws, according to model, secure the brake drum. Remove these and try to pull the brake drum off by hand. If it won't budge, try squirting a little penetrating oil or releasing fluid around the central spigot (where the hub grease cap

sticks through the front of the drum). If the drum still won't come off, you'll have to back off the automatic adjusting mechanism to move the shoes away from the drum.

Three different makes of rear brake have been fitted — study the illustrations to decide which method of releasing the adjusters applies to your car. With the adjusters backed off, the drum should pull off quite easily. You can 'persuade' it if necessary using a soft-faced hammer, or a piece of wood to cushion the

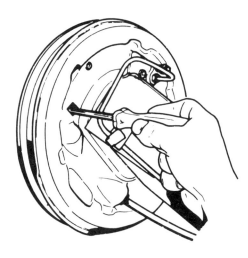

... and release adjuster lever with a screwdriver (Girling brakes)

Remove plug (arrowed) ...

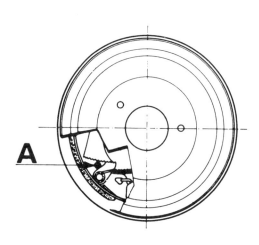

On DBA brakes, press pawl down through hole (A) in backplate

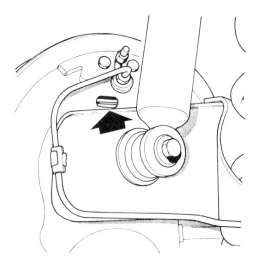

Access hole (arrowed) in Teves brake backplate

Girling rear brake assembly with drum removed. Shoe retainers arrowed

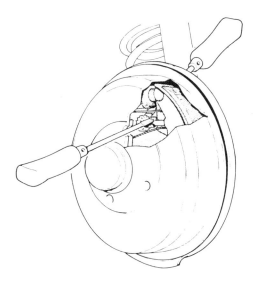

Releasing Teves brakes – release adjuster pawl through wheel bolt hole and rotate nut downwards through backplate hole

blows of a metal hammer. Don't use a metal hammer directly on the drum or you may crack it.

With the brake drum removed, wipe or brush out the dust from the brake drum, brake shoes, and backplate, *but do not inhale it as it is injurious to health.* Scrape any scale or rust from the drum.

Measure the brake shoe lining thickness. If it is worn down to the specified minimum amount, or if it is nearly worn down to the rivets, you will need to renew *all four* brake shoes at the rear. You will also need to renew them (and to fix the leak!) if they are contaminated with grease from a leaking rear hub bearing seal or hydraulic fluid from a leaking wheel cylinder. Renewal of the rear hub seals and wheel cylinder seals is dealt with in the Haynes Owner's Workshop Manual for the Alpine and Solara.

Removal of the brake shoes varies according to type, but the principles are the same. If you've never worked on drum brakes before, take it slowly and only dismantle one side at a time – that way you can study the intact brake assembly if you get stuck during reassembly! A sketch, or even an 'instant' photo, can be a useful memory aid too. If you visit your local accessory shop you'll find various special brake tools on sale – none of these are essential, but some can save a lot of effort. Anyway, here goes:

Girling brakes

Remove the adjuster lever spring, then take the adjuster lever off its pivot. Turn the serrated nut on the

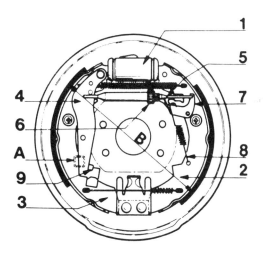

Girling rear brake components

1 Wheel cylinder
2 Leading (primary) shoe
3 Trailing (secondary) shoe
4 Handbrake lever
5 Adjuster pushrod
6 Serrated nut
7 Adjuster lever
8 Spring, adjuster lever
9 Stop, handbrake lever
A Aperture, adjuster release
B Overall diameter of shoes prior to fitting drum
-227 to 227.9mm (8 15/16 to 8 31/32 in)

Releasing the handbrake cable – Girling brakes

drum, then repeat the operations on the other rear wheel.

DBA brakes

Remove the shoe retainers and disconnect the handbrake cable, then lever the bottom ends of the shoes out of the retaining plate. Pull the tops of the shoes out of the wheel cylinder and pull the shoes forwards, taking care not to damage the wheel cylinder boots. Let the shoes move towards the hub so that the springs are slack, unhook the springs and remove the shoes complete with adjuster lever and link rod. Fix a stout rubber band round the wheel cylinder to retain the pistons, and don't let anybody press the brake pedal while the brakes are dismantled.

Remove the spring clips and take off the adjuster lever, link rod and handbrake lever for transferring to

adjuster pushrod to reduce the rod length to the minimum – the left-hand and right-hand units work in opposite directions, so don't get them mixed up.

Take off the shoe retainers (steady pieces) by pushing each retainer inwards with a pair of pliers and turning it anti-clockwise. Withdraw the pins and keep them in a safe place. Push the handbrake lever forwards and unhook the cable end.

Unhook the ends of the lower return spring and lift the bottom end of each shoe out of the retaining plate. Pull the tops of the shoes apart and withdraw them over the wheel cylinder, taking care not to damage the wheel cylinder rubber boots. Don't let anyone press the brake pedal from now on, or the pistons will be pushed out of the wheel cylinder. It's a good idea to put a strong rubber band round the wheel cylinder anyway, in case residual pressure forces the pistons out.

With the shoes removed, unhook the top spring and remove the adjuster pushrod and the handbrake lever for transfer to the new shoes. It's a good idea to use new springs and shoe retainers too – you can get a kit containing all the bits when you buy the brake shoes.

Fit the new shoes in the reverse order to removal, making sure that all the springs go in the right holes. It's not a bad idea to put a smear of brake grease or copper-based anti-seize compound on the shoe-to-backplate rubbing surfaces, pivots and on the adjuster working surfaces. Don't overdo this though, and don't get any grease on the friction linings! (Cover the linings with masking tape if you want, to keep greasy finger-marks off them, but don't forget to remove it when the shoes are back on.) Expand the adjuster pushrod to the point where you can just fit the drum cover over the linings. Refit and secure the brake

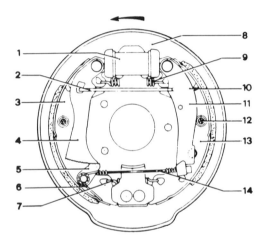

DBA brake components

1	Wheel cylinder
2	Link rod
3	Primary (leading) shoe
4	Adjuster lever
5	Adjuster pawl
6	Adjuster pawl spring
7	Lower shoe return spring
8	Backplate
9	Upper shoe return spring
10	Spring, link rod and handbrake lever
11	Handbrake lever
12	Shoe retainer
13	Secondary (trailing) shoe
14	Handbrake cable

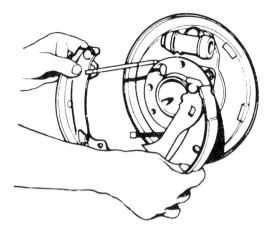

Removing the brake shoes (DBA type)

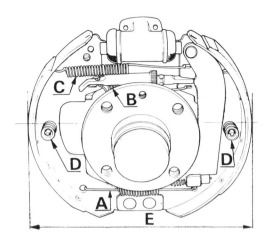

Teves rear brake components

A   Lower return spring
B   Adjuster return spring
C   Upper return spring
D   Shoe retainers
E   Diameter across shoes – 8.98 in (228 mm)

the new shoes. It's a good idea to use new springs and shoe retainers if you're renewing the shoes.

Fit the new shoes in the reverse order to removal. Read the remarks above (for Girling brakes) concerning lubrication and protection of the friction linings. Before refitting the brake drum, push the adjuster lever towards the front shoe and engage the first few teeth with the pawl. Fit and secure the brake drum, then repeat the operations on the other rear wheel.

Teves brakes

The operations are more or less the same as described for Girling brakes, except that the adjuster lever and spring are in a different place. Expand the adjuster pushrod so that the brake drum will just pass over the shoes when reassembling.

All brakes

When both rear brakes have been attended to, start the engine and (with the handbrake released) depress the brake pedal hard twenty or thirty times to operate the automatic adjusters. A clicking sound may be heard from the brakes as this is going on, and the brake pedal travel may reduce. When adjustment seems to be complete, turn your attention to the last item in this schedule . . .

9 Check handbrake adjustment

Adjustment of the handbrake is normally automatic, happening as the rear brake self-adjusting mechanism takes up the wear on the brake linings. As the cable ages and stretches, or after fitting a new cable, adjustment may be necessary. It is carried out as follows.

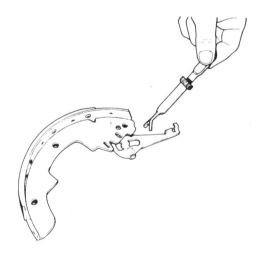

Fitting the adjuster pushrod – Teves brakes

Working under the car, locate the handbrake cable adjuster – it's at the end of the control lever pull-rod. Apply the handbrake lever 5 or 6 clicks, then slacken **77** the locknut and rotate the adjuster nut until the rear wheels are locked. Release the lever and check that the rear wheels are free to rotate, then tighten the locknut.

It's a good idea to lubricate the handbrake cable even if it doesn't need adjusting. Pay particular attention to the places where the cable passes through guides and through the adjuster yoke.

The need for frequent handbrake adjustment may mean that the cable is stretching to the point where it is about to break, or it may mean that the rear brake self-adjusters are not working. Either way, it's a sign that further attention is required.

That's the end of the annual service schedule. By the time you've done all those tasks a couple of times, the next schedule will cause you no problem at all . . .

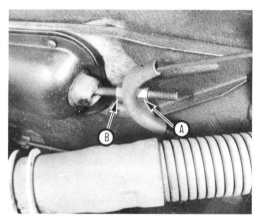

Handbrake cable adjuster nut (A) and locknut (B)

EVERY 20 000 MILES OR EVERY TWO YEARS, WHICHEVER COMES FIRST

In addition to, or instead of, the work specified in the previous schedules

The following additional tools, materials etc may be needed:

Air filter element, in-line fuel filter, gearbox oil.

1 Change manual gearbox/final drive oil

This is listed first because, like the engine oil change, it should ideally be done when the car has just been for a run and the oil has warmed up. The drain plugs for the early type transmission are shown in the illustration accompanying the level checking procedure in the 5000-mile schedule. The later type transmission also has two drain plugs, as you'll see from the diagram herewith. Remove both drain plugs and let the oil drain for at least ten minutes. Remove the filler plug(s) too, it'll speed up the draining.

Refit and tighten the drain plugs – clean them and their seats first if necessary – and refill the transmission and final drive with the correct quantity and grade of oil (see *Vital Statistics* and the lubrication chart). In cold weather you can make the new oil flow more freely by standing the bottle in hot water before using it. Refit the breather/filler plug or filler/level plugs and tighten them when you've filled the transmission and final drive.

2 Renew air filter element

Do this when you've finished mucking out the air cleaner housing. If your car operates in very dusty conditions, more frequent renewal may be advisable. A dirty air cleaner will affect performance and fuel consumption, so don't be tempted to leave the old one in service longer than specified.

Handbrake cable guides

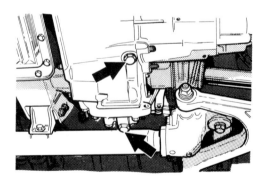

Gearbox and final drive drain plugs (arrowed) – 5-speed model

3 Clean crankcase breather flame trap

The flame trap (also known as an oil separator, from its other function) is that little plastic container with two or three small hoses attached. One of the hoses goes to the air cleaner, the other(s) to the valve cover and/or cylinder block. In time the breather gets clogged up with sludge – this happens more quickly with a well-worn engine – and the operation of the crankcase ventilation system is impaired, possibly resulting in leaking oil seals and increased oil consumption.

Separate the two halves of the flame trap by prising carefully with a screwdriver. (It's probably easiest if you disconnect at least one of the hoses first.) Take out the filter discs and clean them in paraffin. Clean out the flame trap body while you're at it; if the hoses are full of sludge, take them off and clean them out or renew them. If there is a lot of 'mayonnaise' present – a whitish mixture of oil and water – this may be caused by the engine not warming up properly, due either to lots of short journeys or to the cooling system thermostat being stuck open.

When everything's clean and dry, put the filter discs back into the flame trap housing and snap the two halves together. Renew the flame trap if you can't get the discs clean. Reconnect the hoses too.

4 Renew in-line fuel filter

When fitted, this useful item is plumbed into the fuel line between the fuel pump and the carburettor. It cannot be cleaned, but must be renewed periodically. On models with power steering, the filter is bolted to the back of the steering pump.

Take off the hose clips and pull the hoses off the filter, then fit the new one, making sure that the arrow (if there is one) on the filter body points in the direction of fuel flow, ie towards the carburettor. Tighten the hose clips – use new clips if you mangled the old ones getting them off, and use new hoses for that matter if the old ones look tatty. Check for leaks when you next run the engine.

That's about the end of the DIY jobs in this schedule. There is one more thing to be done, but you'll probably have to get your garage or friendly expert to do it – namely:

5 Check rear hub bearing adjustment and correct if necessary

You can at least check this yourself. Jack up each rear wheel in turn (front wheels chocked, handbrake off) and try to rock the wheel, gripping it at top and bottom, then at each side. There should be very little or no play. Spin the wheel and listen for rumbling or

Arrow on fuel filter must point towards carburettor

grinding noises, which may be warning you of impending bearing trouble. (On the road, a worn wheel bearing on the right-hand side will make most noise on a left-hand bend but quieten down completely on a right-hander, and vice versa.)

If adjustment is necessary, indicated by excessive slack in the bearing, take the car to the garage or to your mechanically proficient friend, who will have a torque wrench and a knowledge of the procedures involved. Or invest in a torque wrench and a copy of the Haynes Owner's Workshop Manual for the Alpine and Solara, and become your own expert!

EVERY 40 000 MILES OR EVERY FOUR YEARS, WHICHEVER COMES FIRST

In addition to, or instead of, the work specified in the previous schedules

The following additional tools or materials may be required:

Brake servo air filter.

1 Repack rear hub bearings with grease

We've put this first in order to avoid repeating the remarks made in the previous schedule concerning hub adjustment. They apply equally to this job. It's one of those tasks which needs doing so infrequently that in practice it never gets done – and the same could be said of the next item:

2 Renew brake servo air filter

The 'official' way of doing this job involves removing the servo unit from the car, which is a bit **79**

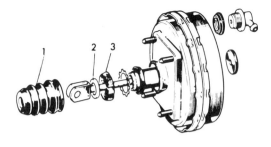

Brake servo air filter details

1   *Rubber boot*
2   *Filter retainer*
3   *Air filter*

PREVENTIVE MAINTENANCE — BRAKING SYSTEM

Because brake fluid absorbs water from the air, it gradually deteriorates and the water may attack other braking system components. For this reason, it is recommended that every two years, regardless of mileage, the brake fluid is drained and renewed with fresh fluid. One of the pressure bleeding kits available in DIY motor shops is an invaluable aid for this job. Follow the instructions supplied with the kit.

For the same reason, every four years, when renewing the brake fluid, have all rubber seals and hoses renewed at the same time. This is also a good opportunity to renew any damaged or corroded steel brake pipes.

This may seem like an expensive piece of preventive maintenance, but it's better than having a brake seal or hose fail in an emergency stop! In any case, it's not a job for the inexperienced mechanic. Study the Haynes Owner's Workshop Manual for the Alpine and Solara if you think you're up to it; otherwise leave it to your Talbot dealer.

SEASONAL SERVICING

If you carry out the procedures we've detailed so far, at more or less the prescribed intervals of mileage or time, then you'll have gone a long way towards getting the best out of your Alpine or Solara in terms both of performance and long life. That's the good news. The other kind is that there are always other areas, not dealt with in regular servicing schedules, where neglect can spell trouble.

We reckon a bit of extra time spent on your car at the beginning and end of the winter will be well repaid in terms of peace of mind and prevention of trouble. The suggested attentions which follow have therefore been divided into Spring and Autumn sections — but there's nothing to prevent you doing them more frequently if you like!

SPRING

We've put this one first as it's less depressing than Autumn — though there's probably more work involved!

Check air cleaner seasonal setting

You may have noticed the lever on the air cleaner pick-up box. It can be moved to one of three positions: 'ETE' (Summer), 'HIVER' (Winter) and an intermediate position. The intermediate position is probably correct for most of the year in England, since it should be used at an air temperature of between 41° and 68° F (5° and 20° C). Above or below these

beyond the scope of this book. If you don't mind doing fiddly work in cramped conditions, though, you can renew the filter as follows.

Move the front seats back as far as possible and get down on the floor of the car with your torch or inspection light. Disconnect the servo pushrod from the brake pedal arm — it's held by a fastening known as a clevis pin and a sort of hairgrip spring clip, which will play hell with your fingernails if you're not careful. Pull the rubber boot back — if possible, work it off the end of the pushrod, otherwise just roll it back. Use a piece of bent wire, or a crochet hook, to pull the filter and retainer out of the servo. Either slide them off the end of the rod and slide the new filter on, or make a diagonal cut in the old filter to withdraw it and fit the new filter in a similar fashion. Push the filter and retainer home, wriggle the rubber boot back into position and reconnect the brake pedal clevis.

3 Change automatic transmission fluid (when applicable)

The makers say that the ATF should be changed every 30 000 miles if the car is used under adverse conditions (mainly short journeys, much towing, or climatic extremes) but that it's not otherwise necessary to change it. If you want to change yours — and it's not a bad idea after this mileage, regardless of operating conditions — it's another dealer or expert job. The transmission sump has to be removed to drain the fluid, an interval filter has to be cleaned or renewed, and an adjustment or two has to be made at the end of it. Again, you find all the details in the

Haynes Owner's Workshop Manual.

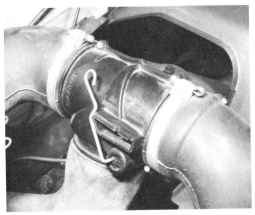

Air cleaner seasonal adjustment lever

contamination. After all the brushing and scraping, a final wash down with the hose will remove the last of the dirt and mud.

You can now check for leaks in the floor; if you find any, dry the area carefully, then use a mastic type sealer to plug the offending gap. Hollow sections of doors and bodywork can be sprayed or brush-painted with a rust-inhibitor to provide some extra protection. If there are signs of the underseal breaking away, this is a good opportunity to patch it up. Undersealing paint is available in spray cans or tins from accessory shops; one small point about putting the stuff on though, and that's to make sure the area is clean and dry, otherwise you're wasting your time.

While you're underneath, have a good look round for signs of rusting. Likely places are the body sills, floor panels and wings, and if you do find any rust have a word with the local Talbot man or body repair shop before things get too bad.

Bodywork

This too will have suffered from all the muck and salt that's around during the winter, and there's no better time to wash it thoroughly and check for stone chips and rust spots. You're bound to find some, despite the regular washing you've given the car – or meant to – throughout the winter. Treat as for rusty scratches (see *Body Beautiful*).

After the touch-up paint has thoroughly hardened, it's worth giving the car a good polish to prepare it for the long, hot summer ahead (well, there's no harm in hoping). If you're feeling really energetic you could do the interior as well (*Body Beautiful* again) but the most important cleaning jobs are now done.

temperatures, use the Summer or Winter positions respectively.

Underside of car

In Spring, we venture to suggest, the owner's fancy lightly turns to thoughts of cleaning off all the accumulated muck of winter from underneath the car. Without a shadow of doubt, the best time to clean underneath is the worst time from the discomfort point of view – that is, when the car's been driven in the wet and all the dirt's nicely softened up. So let's talk first about the easiest way out – steam cleaning or pressure washing. These are not DIY jobs, and can only be done at larger garages, usually those which undertake body repair jobs. You may feel this method's unnecessarily expensive, but it's generally preferable to grovelling about underneath and getting filthy and uncomfortable doing it yourself. However, for the owner who really wants to do it by hand, here goes . . .

You'll need paraffin or a water-soluble solvent, water (and preferably a hose), a wire brush, a scraper and a stiff bristle brush.

To start with, jack the car up as high as possible, preferably at one side or one end. For your own safety, support it on ramps or concrete/wooden blocks and chock the wheels which are on the ground. Unless all the wheels are raised, also apply the handbrake; and engage first or reverse gear.

Now get underneath (you've put it off as long as you can!) and cover the brake discs and calipers with polythene bags to stop mud and water getting into them. Next loosen any encrusted dirt and, working from one end or one side, scrape or brush it away. The paraffin or solvent can be used where there's oil

AUTUMN

With winter on the way, your car's electrical system is going to take much more of a beating than it has during the last few months. Now – and not on a dark night miles from anywhere in a snowstorm – is the time to check the vital components.

Lights

Check operation.

Renew any failed bulbs or check for faults as necessary.

Wipers/washers

These are going to get a lot of use, so check the wiper arms and blades. Top up the washer reservoir and check operation.

Radiator antifreeze mustn't be used in the screenwash system as it's harmful to paintwork. Special additives can be obtained for the screenwash **81**

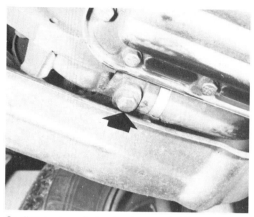

Cooling system drain plug (arrowed). Disconnect the hose to drain if no drain plug is fitted

Radiator filler cap – remove for draining and refilling only

reservoir to prevent freezing up during winter.

Cooling system

Check that the antifreeze solution in the engine cooling system's of the correct strength or, if there's no antifreeze in, add some. 'Bluecol' antifreeze or equivalent is recommended and can be left in the cooling system for up to two years. If you have antifreeze in already but are uncertain of its strength, it's advisable to have the specific gravity of the coolant checked by your garage.

Every other year you should drain the cooling system, flush it out by running water through it until it comes out clean, then refill with fresh antifreeze mixture. Have the heater controls set for maximum heat when you do this, and do the flushing and filling through the radiator filler – the one that says 'DO NOT REMOVE' on it.

It's a good idea to think about renewing the cooling system rubber hoses when you change the coolant. They don't last for ever, and fresh antifreeze has a disconcerting ability to seek out little cracks.

If your car has a bleed plug on the thermostat elbow – where the radiator top hose joins the cylinder head – the plug should be removed when draining and flushing the system, and left out when refilling until coolant starts to flow out of it. On all models, fill up via the radiator filler hole until coolant is up to the bottom of the hole, then refit the plug and top up the expansion bottle. Run the engine until it has warmed up and bubbles have ceased to appear in the expansion bottle, then allow the engine to cool and top up again if necessary.

Air cleaner

Don't forget to alter the seasonal setting once the weather gets cold.

Tyres

Check tread and condition. Remember that you may well be driving in slippery conditions.

Useful aerosols

When next at your local garage or accessory shop it's a good idea to get a can of ignition waterproofer, and you'll probably need a can of windscreen de-icer at your disposal sometime during the coming winter months. These items should be carried in the car so that they're always on hand when needed in damp or icy conditions.

Bodywork

Finally, if you've got any energy left, wash the car and polish it thoroughly to help protect the paint against the winter elements.

Body Beautiful

If you've bought this book intending to do all the routine servicing of your car yourself, then you'll surely want to keep the bodywork and inside of the car looking good too. For anyone who doesn't, here's how to do it anyway . . .

Some people regard car cleaning as one of the joyful aspects of ownership, others look on it as a tedious task and a necessary evil. If you fall into the latter category, then the best plan of action is to do a little each week, dividing the job into sections. In this way you'll at least maintain a reasonable standard of appearance and break up the monotony of the job.

The really keen types won't only have the interior and bodywork dazzling, but will also keep the engine free of oil and dirt. Though you may be horrified at the idea, it's not a bad one when you think about it. For one thing, if you do carry out any repairs on the engine or surrounding components, the job will be made that much easier and more pleasant just because you'll keep yourself cleaner and be able to see what you're doing. Another point is that any oil or water leaks can easily be traced at an early stage and rectified before they get really serious.

It is not suggested that the car be thoroughly washed and cleaned from all angles every weekend by the average owner, but rather more on a seasonal basis, combined with (say) the Spring and Autumn service checks. Other than this, all that will be required will be a quick weekly wash and leather of the paintwork and a quick brushing-out of the interior.

It's always a good idea to clean the interior first; this way you won't get the dust all over your nicely polished exterior – or the car's! Begin by removing all the contents, not forgetting the odds and ends in the pockets and glovebox. Then take out all the mats and carpets, which should be shaken and brushed, or better still vacuum-cleaned. If they need further cleaning this can be done with a carpet shampoo, but let them dry thoroughly before you put them back. Any underfelt should be taken out and shaken, too, but don't try washing this or it may end up in rather more pieces than you started with.

If the carpets should just happen to be in such a bad state of decay that they don't merit cleaning, why

not get yourself a decent set of replacements? You can get kits tailored for your particular model from specialist firms, and they're quite reasonably priced.

The inside of the car can now be cleaned with a brush and dustpan, or again preferably, a vacuum-cleaner. If the flex on the Hoover won't stretch to the car (and the car won't squeeze through the front door!) it might be worth thinking about investing in one of the small 12-volt hand vacuums which can be attached to your car battery – your accessory shop can probably show you one.

Seat and trim materials can be wiped over with warm water containing a little washing-up liquid, but for best results (particularly if they're very dirty) use one of the proprietary upholstery cleaners, which are specially made for the job. An old nail brush will help to remove ingrained marks, but don't splash too much water about and do wipe the surfaces dry afterwards with a clean cloth, leaving the windows open to speed up drying. The carpets can be put back when they're quite dry, making sure they're properly fitted around the controls etc.

You have to be careful about cleaning car windows, especially the windscreen, with some household products as these can leave a smeary film. Water containing a few drops of ammonia is probably best, but any stubborn marks and smears can be removed with methylated spirit; finish off with a chamois leather squeezed as dry as possible.

Just in case you should think that's it, there's still the luggage area to be dealt with. Take out that collection of junk that seems to have grown every time you open the tailgate or boot lid, and get busy with brush or vacuum cleaner again. While you're at it, if you must carry all that stuff around, now's the time to try and stow it so it doesn't rattle any more!

Now you can pause for a moment – make a well-earned cup of tea perhaps – and take a critical look at the interior. Are there any nicks or tears in the seats or **83** other trim? Is the headlining drooping or peeling? Some excellent products can now be obtained for repairs such as these. One of the most useful is probably the vinyl repair kit, which comes in various colours and consists of a quantity of 'liquid vinyl' and some sheets of texturing material. The liquid's applied to a split or hole in a plastic seat or piece of trim, smoothed like body filler, and allowed to set. It's then blended into the surrounding area by selecting the best matching pattern from the graining material supplied, placing this over the repair and rubbing with a hot iron; the pattern's then embossed into the repaired area.

For larger splits or tears it may be necessary to cut a piece of matching material from somewhere that doesn't show, apply some suitable adhesive to it and work it under the edges of the tear, pressing these together as neatly as possible once the glue has become tacky enough. Any loose headlining or trim can also be stuck in place – but make sure you get an adhesive that's suitable for PVC or vinyl.

The cropped nylon type of upholstery should be cleaned by brushing and then wiping over with a lightly dampened cloth.

Once you've got the seats in a reasonable state of cleanliness and repair, why not consider seat covers? Like carpets, they're available from specialist firms to suit your car and are a worthwhile buy in view of the protection they give.

If you use your car regularly and you've got the time and inclination, it should really be washed every week either by hand (preferably using a hosepipe) or by taking advantage of the local car-wash if there is one. Whichever method you choose (assuming you wash your car at all!) we don't think we need tell you how to do it – but remember it's never a good idea to just wipe over a very dirty car, whether wet or dry; you might as well sandpaper it!

Two or three times a year (even once is better than not at all) a good silicone or wax polish can be used on the paintwork. We don't know which of the many makes you'll use, so we can only recommend you to follow the makers' instructions closely so that you do see a reward for your efforts. Chrome parts are best cleaned with a special chrome cleaner; ordinary metal polish will attack the finish

If the paint's beginning to lose its gloss or colour, and ordinary polishing doesn't seem to help, it will be worth considering the use of a polish with a mild 'cutting' action to remove what is, in effect, a surface layer of dead paint. Your friendly neighbourhood accessory shop man will advise on a suitable type.

The remainder of this Chapter describes how to keep your car's bodywork and paintwork in good condition by dealing with scratches and more major

damage too, as they occur. A number of repair aids and materials are referred to, most of them essential if you're to achieve good results. They should all be available, together with free advice, from good motor accessory shops. Before repairing any paint or bodywork remember that the success of the work lies in the preparation.

Keeping paintwork up to scratch

With superficial scratches (the sort other people seem to get) where they don't penetrate down to the metal you'll be glad to hear that repair can be very simple. Lightly rub the area with a paintwork renovator or a fine cutting paste to remove any loose paint from the scratch and to clean off any polish. Rinse the area with plenty of clean water and allow to dry. Apply touch-up paint to the scratch using a fine brush, and continue to build up the paint by several applications, allowing each to dry, until it's level with the surrounding area. Allow the new paint at least two weeks to harden (knitting or a crossword puzzle will help to pass the time) then use the paint renovator or cutting paste again to blend it into the original. Now a good polish can be used.

When you've got a scratch that's penetrated right through to the metal, causing rusting, you need a different technique. Use your scout knife to remove any loose rust from the bottom of the scratch, then paint on a rust-inhibiting paint to prevent it from spreading. You'll probably now need to apply cellulose body stopper paste – use a rubber or nylon applicator or a knife, but don't borrow one from the kitchen as you'll have a job cleaning it.

The paste can be thinned down if necessary using cellulose thinners. Before it hardens, it's a good idea to wrap a piece of smooth cotton rag round the end of your finger, dip it in thinners and quickly sweep it across the filled scratch. This ensures that the area's very slightly hollowed and allows the paint to be built up to the correct level as described earlier.

Dealing with dents

When your car's bodywork gets a deep depression, you'll probably have one too. But there's no reason why even fairly large dents can't be tackled successfully by the DIY owner, especially using the excellent body repair materials now available. So cheer up, and let's see what can be done.

The first step is to try to pull the dented metal out to bring it more or less back to the original level. Don't expect to make a perfect job of this – you won't; the metal has stretched and 'work-hardened' which makes it a virtually impossible job. Try to bring the level up to about $\frac{1}{8}$ inch below the surrounding area; obviously, with shallow dents you can bypass this bit.

If the underside of the dent can be got at, try hammering it out gently from behind, using a hammer with a wooden or plastic head. You'll need to hold a fairly heavy hardwood block on the outside of the dent; this absorbs the impact of the hammer blows and helps to stop the metal being dented in the opposite direction!

If you've got a dent in a completely enclosed body section, or there's something else preventing you from getting behind it, a different approach is needed. Try to screw up enough courage to drill several small holes through the metal in the dent, particularly in the deeper parts. Now screw in several self-tapping screws so that they get a good bite, and either pull on the heads with pliers or wrap some heavy gauge steel wire round them and pull this. Brace yourself in case something gives suddenly or you may dent your own bodywork!

Now to remove the paint from the damaged area. This is best done using a power drill and abrasive paper. Don't forget to remove the paint from an inch or so of the surrounding good paintwork, too, so that everything blends in nicely. Now score the metal surface with a screwdriver or the tang of a file to provide a good key for the filler which you're going to have to apply. To finish off the repair, refer to the 'Filling and Spraying' section later on.

Rust holes and gashes

If there's any paint left on the affected area, remove it as described previously so that you can get a good idea of just how bad the problem is. If there's more rust or fresh air than good metal, now's the time to consider whether a replacement panel would be more appropriate; this is a body shop job, beyond the scope of this book.

If things don't seem that bad and you're prepared to have a go at doing the job yourself, remove all the fittings from the surrounding area except those which may help to give a good guide to what the shape should be (eg headlamp shells). Now, get a hacksaw blade or a pair of snips and cut out all the loose and badly affected metal. Hammer the edges inwards so that you've got a recessed area to build up on.

Wire brush the edges to remove any powdery rust, then paint over with a rust inhibitor; if you can get to the back, do the same to that. You're now going to fill the hole with something, but unfortunately just anything won't do. The best bets are zinc gauze or aluminium tape. The gauze is probably the favourite for a large hole. Cut a piece slightly larger than the hole to be filled, then position it in the hole so that its edges are below the level of the surrounding bodywork. If necessary, hold it in place with a few blobs of filler paste. For small or narrow holes you can use the aluminium tape which is sold by the roll. Pull off a piece and trim to the approximate size and shape required. If there's backing paper, peel it off (it sticks better that way) and place the tape over the hole; if necessary, pieces can be overlapped at the edges. Burnish down the edges of the tape with a file handle or similar to make sure it's firmly adhering to the metal.

With the hole now blocked off, the affected area can be filled and sprayed as follows.

Filling and spraying

Many types of body filler are available, but generally speaking those proprietary kits which contain filler paste (or a filler powder and resin liquid) and a separate hardener are best. You'll also need a flexible plastic or nylon applicator (usually supplied) for putting the mixture on with. Mix up a little of the filler on a piece of board or plastic (those plastic margarine tubs are ideal but do wash out all traces of the contents first!). Read the instructions carefully and don't make up too much at one go. You'll find you have to work fairly fast or the mixture will begin to set, especially if you've been a bit generous with the hardener.

Apply the paste to the prepared hole or dent more or less to the correct level and contour, but don't try to shape it once it's become tacky or it'll pick up on the applicator. Layers should be built up at intervals until the final level's just proud of the surrounding bodywork.

When the filler's fully hardened, use a Surform plane or coarse file to remove the excess and obtain the final shape. Then follow with progressively finer grades of wet-or-dry abrasive paper starting with coarse, followed by medium, then fine (some manufacturers give 'grit' grade to their wet-or-dry paper — 40 is the coarsest, 400 the finest you will probably need). Always wrap the paper round a block if you're trying to get a flat surface, and keep it wet by rinsing in clean water, or the filler and paint will clog up the abrasive surface.

At this point, the doctored area should be surrounded by a ring of bare metal, encircled by a feathered edge of good paintwork. Rinse it with plenty of clean water to get rid of all the paint and filler dust and allow it to dry completely.

If you're happy with the surface you've obtained then you're ready to apply some paint. First spray over the whole area with a light coat of grey primer. This will show up any surface imperfections which may need further treatment, and will also help you get the knack of spraying with an aerosol can before you start on the colour coats. Rub down the surface again, and if necessary use a little body stopper, as described for **85**

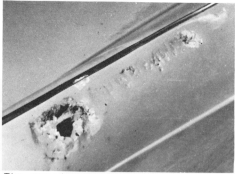

The procedure given with these photos is simplified; more comprehensive instructions will be found in the accompanying text. Typical rust damage is shown here, but the procedure for the repair of dents and gashes is similar.

First remove fittings from the immediate area and then remove loose rust and paint. A wire brush or abrasive disc mounted in a power drill is best, although the job can be done by hand. You need to be very thorough.

The edges of a hole should be tapped inwards with a hammer to provide a hollow for the filler. Having done this, apply rust inhibitor to the affected area (including the underside where possible) and allow this to dry thoroughly.

Before attempting to fill larger holes, block them off with suitable material. Metal tape can be used, but the picture shows a piece of aluminium gauze being sized up for use on this hole.

When mixing the body filler, follow the manufacturers' instructions very carefully. Mix thoroughly, don't mix too much at one go, and don't make it up until you're ready to start filling - modern fillers begin to harden very quickly!

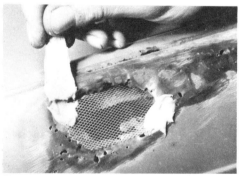

The tape or gauze used for backing up a hole can be secured in position with a few small blobs of filler paste. It's a good idea to mix a very small quantity for this purpose first.

After mixing the filler, apply it quickly with a flexible applicator, following the contours of the body. The filler should be built up in successive thin layers, the final one being just above the level of the surrounding bodywork.

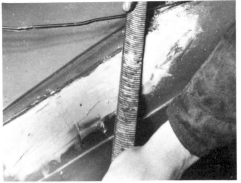

A fairly coarse file or cutting tool is best for removing excess filler and for achieving the initial contour. Care must be taken not to overdo the filing or you'll hollow out the surface and have to fill it again!

A sanding block will now be needed; this can be made of wood as shown or a purpose-made rubber one can be purchased. Begin shaping the filler by using the block with progressively finer grades of dry abrasive paper, followed by …

… wet and-dry paper, keeping both the work area and the paper wet. Rubbing down is complete when the filled area is 'feathered' into the surrounding painted areas, as shown; this final stage is achieved with the finest grade paper.

After thorough washing and drying, any necessary masking can be done and a coat of primer applied. Again, build this up with successive thin layers. Once the primer is dry it should be smoothed with very fine wet-and-dry paper.

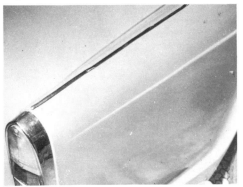

The top coat of paint can now be applied, again in thin layers. Later a mild cutting paste can be used to blend it with the surrounding paint. Finish off with a good quality polish.

minor scratches, to fill any small imperfections. Repeat this spray-and-level procedure until you're satisfied with the finish; then wash down again and allow to dry.

The next stage is to apply the finishing coats, but first a word or two about the techniques involved. Paint spraying should be done in a warm, dry, windless, dust-free atmosphere — conditions not very readily available to most of us! You may be able to duplicate them artificially if you've got a large indoor workshop, but if you have to work outside you'll need to pick the day carefully. If you're working in your garage you'll probably need to 'lay' the dust on the floor by damping it with water.

If the body repair's confined to a small patch, mask off the surrounding area to protect it from paint spray. Bodywork fittings (chrome strips, or door handles and the like) will need to be either masked or removed. If you're masking, use genuine masking tape and plenty of newspaper as necessary. Before starting to spray, shake the aerosol can thoroughly; then experiment on something (an old tin or similar will do — not the neighbours' car) until you feel you can apply the paint smoothly. At the previous stage this wasn't too important, but now you're trying to get the best possible finish.

First cover the repair area with a thick coat of primer — not as one coat, but built up of several thin ones. When this is dry, using the finest wet-or-dry paper, rub down the surface until it's really smooth. Use plenty of water to keep the surface clean; when it's dry, spray on another primer coat and repeat the procedure.

Now for the top coat. Again the idea's to build up the paint thickness by several thin coats. Have a test spray first as this is a different aerosol, then commence spraying in the centre of the repair area. Using a circular motion, work gradually outwards towards the edges until the whole of the repair and about two inches of the surrounding paint is covered. Remove all the masking material 10 to 15 minutes after you've finished spraying.

Now you can start putting away all the bits and pieces because it'll need about two weeks for the paint to harden completely. After this time, using a paint renovator or a very fine cutting paste, blend the edges of the new paint into the original. Finally, apply a good wax or silicone polish, and hopefully you'll have a repair which is only noticeable by its absence!

Adding 'Pinstripes'

There are various kinds of self-adhesive body decor available for customising your car, while some models have their own side-stripes built in. Perhaps the neatest and most suitable of the 'add-on' variety are Pinstripes, and we've included these in this Chapter as they may appeal to the owner who wants a cheap and simple way to improve the appearance of his or her car. They're adhesive tapes which come in different widths and colours and as single or multi-stripes. Most have a backing paper which is peeled off as the stripe is applied.

When applying any of these self-adhesive tapes, first make sure the paintwork's clean by washing with warm water and a car shampoo or liquid detergent. Next clean up the surface with a very fine cutting paste or paintwork renovator, and wash down again. You can now apply the tape, but follow the directions carefully. Smooth it down with a clean rag and, if necessary, prick out any small air bubbles with a pin. Try not to stretch the stripes as you put them on because they'll shrink slightly anyway; and wrap the ends round the panels so that they don't pull away at the edges.

Upholstery painting

If you think the upholstery or interior panelling of your car requires renovating, or maybe you want to improve the colour scheme or make it look more sporty, there are various colours of upholstery paint available in accessory shops. You can also use the paint to cover up repairs, but make sure it's a perfect match or you could make things look worse. Of course you shouldn't try to paint fabric upholstery or trim!

The Personal Touch

On the subject of accessories it's been said that, if someone else makes it, the motorist will buy it. The 'after-market' in extras and accessories has now grown to enormous proportions, you only need to browse through a car magazine or motor accessory shop to see what we mean. The problem for any motorist is to sort out the useful and practical items from what, at the other end of the scale, is some undoubted rubbish.

The subject of accessories is so broad that in a Handbook like this we can only 'touch the tip of the iceberg' so we've tried to cover just a few of the more popular accessories and to include some tips on fitting where appropriate.

All good products will be supplied with general fitting instructions which may or may not require minor modifications to suit your Alpine or Solara. If you're buying secondhand, of course, you may get no instructions at all. The guidelines given here are in no way intended to replace the manufacturers' instructions, and if you're in doubt about fitting a particular item, they're the people to refer to.

Note: *Always disconnect the battery before commencing any work involving the electrical system.* Fireworks are very pretty, but there's a time and place for everything.

Auxiliary instruments

It would be possible to write a complete book on auxiliary instruments and how to fit them but, as with other things, you'll normally get pretty good instructions when you buy them. Because there are so many instruments available, we're only going to consider battery condition indicators, clocks, oil pressure gauges, tachometers and vacuum gauges.

First of all, even before you've decided what instruments you're going to fit, you've got to think where to fit them. The dash panel doesn't lend itself readily to fitting brackets and small extra panels. If you do decide to put anything there, make sure there's nothing immediately behind the mounting point because you'll have to drill and file out a suitable hole. Some instruments such as tachometers can be 'pod' types which are surface mounted. Another answer may be a central console, which will not only allow you to mount instruments but may have a radio installation compartment and/or a storage pocket. Some information on these is given later on.

Sooner or later you're going to have to start drilling some holes somewhere, but this needn't cause any real headaches if it's approached in the right way. As already mentioned, make sure there's nothing behind the panel before even considering drilling a hole, and that there's enough room to fit the instrument, switch, or whatever, in the space chosen. Any hole which will have a cable or capillary running through it must have a plastic or rubber grommet to prevent the metal chafing through; these grommets can be obtained from DIY accessory or car electrical shops.

When it comes to drilling larger holes for instruments, start off by centre-punching the middle of the area, then use compasses or dividers to mark the hole, allowing a little for clearance (standard instruments are 2 in/52 mm diameter). It's best to mark another hole inside the first hole, and drill around this line so that the centre part can readily be pushed out; if you're using a ⅛ in drill the inner circle will need to be ⅛ in inside the first circle marked. Finish the job off carefully filing and deburring the hole.

An alternative method of cutting large holes is to use a tank cutter of the type used by plumbers. Some of these, which resemble a circular hacksaw blade, can be purchased in a variety of diameters and will fit in an electric drill, so removing much of the hard work.

Battery condition indicator

The battery condition indicator's simply a voltmeter, and as such must be connected to a good earth point on the body and to any suitable connection which is live when the ignition switch is ON. For convenience, this could be a wire attached to **89**

Some of the supplementary instruments and other accessories available from Smiths Industries

the ignition switch or fuse box. You don't need heavy cables for the battery condition indicator, 14/0.30 mm (14/.012 in) should be OK, but make sure the earth polarity's correct.

Clock

Most models have a clock fitted when new, but owners of the downrange variants may wish to add a clock to their more basic model.

Clocks come in many forms, you can even get car clocks powered by dry cell batteries. Most car clocks which are wired to the car's power source contain semiconductors. If this means nothing else to you, it should mean that there's a negligible load on the battery and that the polarity's critical if you don't want to cause permanent damage. Connections are much the same as the battery condition indicator except that you don't want the clock to stop when the ignition's switched off. Therefore connect the feed wire to a fuse which is permanently live.

Tachometer

The tachometer (rev counter) is the one instrument that's available in larger sizes than the others (80 mm instead of 52 mm, although the smaller size can be obtained). Most are positive *or* negative earth, but you must connect them up correctly. In case you should pick up a secondhand one, connections for the most common types are shown in the illustrations. Note that with the Smiths type, the distributor-to-coil LT lead is removed; also note the sleeve colours on the main white lead. Use a 14/0.30 (14/.012) cable size.

Oil pressure gauge

Oil pressure gauges may have an electrical sender unit, similar in appearance to the water temperature gauge sender, or a capillary tube which carries a thin column of oil up to the gauge head. Either way, connection is made using a T-piece (usually supplied with the gauge) screwed into the oil pressure switch

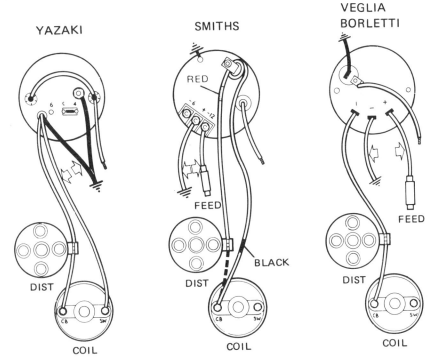

YAZAKI

SMITHS

VEGLIA BORLETTI

Connections for three popular tachometers

Yazaki: Negative earth shown – reverse arrowed wires to change polarity
Smiths: Positive earth shown – the dotted connection must be removed when the tachometer is fitted. Reverse arrowed wires to change polarity
Veglia Borletti: Negative earth shown – reverse arrowed wires to change polarity

tapping, which is located just below No 1 spark plug. The existing warning light switch screws into one arm of the T, and the gauge sender or pipe union into the other arm.

With the electrical type of gauge, connections must be made to an ignition-controlled live point, to the instrument lighting circuit, and to earth, as well as to the sender unit itself. The mechanical type of gauge will only need the lighting and earth connections.

Vacuum gauge (performance gauge or fuel consumption gauge)

This is simply a suction (negative pressure) gauge which screws into a tapping on the inlet manifold, with a flexible pipe for the meter. Once you've got the hang of using it, it can be very useful as an aid to economical driving. The only tricky bit about installation is making a tapping point in the manifold. You may be able to use a T-piece in the brake servo vacuum line; otherwise, get advice from your local garage or from the place where you buy the gauge.

Consoles

Consoles come in all shapes, sizes and prices. Before buying, have a good look round to see what's

Oil pressure warning light switch

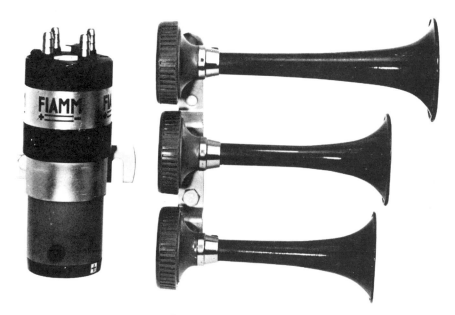

Fiamm 'Trio' air horns

on the market – that includes looking through the motoring DIY magazines. Some types extend back from the engine compartment wall or dash panel to behind the handbrake, the handbrake and gear levers coming up through the console base panel. You get them with cut-outs for switches, radios and tape players, and for the standard 52 mm diameter circular instruments. Many types also have an ashtray or storage pocket, some also have an arm-rest; there's even a type that fits to the roof! They come in a variety of finishes – black leatherette, fibreglass, or wood-grain, and in various colours. Without a great deal of difficulty you should be able to get something that suits both your taste and your pocket.

Fitting of consoles is usually straightforward, but you may need to drill a few holes which could lead to your buying some self-tapping screws as well. Before drilling, don't forget to look what's on the other side of the panel, or your 'extra' could prove extra expensive!

Warning devices

Air horns

Air horns are marketed by several companies as a DIY installation kit comprising the horns themselves, a compressor unit, a relay, plastic piping and electrical cable. What you've obviously got to do is mount the horns reasonably near the compressor, and the compressor reasonably near the relay, or the connections just won't reach. It's normal for the manufacturers to specify a certain way up for the compressor to be mounted, but there shouldn't be any other problems. You'll need to make sure that the electrical connections are as per the maker's instructions for the relay and compressor, and decide whether you want to use the air horns in conjunction with, or in place of, the original car horn. If you have to connect into existing wiring, make sure the connections are well made and, if these involve soldering, don't forget to insulate any soldered joints.

Child safety seats and harnesses

Much has been said in recent years about the use of seat belts for front seat passengers, and more recently there's been an increasing interest in the various special rear seats and harnesses now available for babies and younger children. It's not possible to give specific instructions for fitting these, because there are so many types around, but what you must be careful about is ensuring that you buy a BSI-approved type.

Most types have a pair of straps at the lower edge which need to be attached to the rear seat pan at the back of the squab, and a further pair of straps that fit over the back of the car seat for attachment to the floor or wheel arch. Take very careful note of the manufacturer's instructions; they require the anchorages to be a certain distance apart, and may also

KL's Jeenay child safety seat

require reinforcing plates to be used. Before starting to drill holes for the mountings, make sure the underside or rear of the panel's clear of obstructions, pipes or any other components.

Lamps

When auxiliary lamps are fitted, not only must you fit them in a suitable place on the car, but you must also meet certain legal requirements; where these apply we've attempted to give some guidelines.

Spot and front fog lamps

It's illegal to mount these with the lower edge of the illuminating surface *more than* 1200 mm (47.24 in) from the ground. Any lamps that are mounted with this lower edge *less than* 500 mm (19.69 in) above the ground may only be used in fog or falling snow. In conditions where the law requires headlamps to be used, eg at night on a unlit road, a *single* lamp may be used only *in conjunction with* the headlamps. In these conditions the lamps must always be mounted and used *in pairs* (two fog, two spot or one of each) if they're used as spotlamps, they should conform to the normal anti-dazzle requirements, eg by wiring them so that they go out when the headlamps are dipped, or by angling them slightly downwards.

Choose the lamps carefully, and if possible match the lamp styles. There are many good types on sale, so if you're not sure what you want ask for advice. The actual mounting is not too difficult; they can either be fitted to a bumper bracket or attached by a separate bracket to the front grille.

To prevent overloading of the existing wiring, a relay should be used (the Lucas 6RA type, part No 33213, is suitable). This is connected through the switch from the existing headlamp circuit to one of the relay 'coil' terminals, with the other terminal being connected either to the battery or the battery connection at the starter solenoid, via a line fuse. The fuse rating will depend on the lamp manufacturers' recommendations, but will probably be about 20 amps for a pair of lamps.

Rear fog lamps

Under the Road Vehicles (Rear Fog Lamps) Regulations 1978, the fitting of at least one rear fog lamp became compulsory on cars manufactured on or after October 1, 1979 and first used on or after April 1, 1980. These same regulations lay down specific rules on the use and positioning of such lamps.

Either one or two lamps may be fitted. If only one is used, it must be on the centre line or to the offside of the car, and at least 100 mm (3.94 in) from the nearest brake light. No rear fog lamp is to be illuminated by the braking system of the car. The rear fog lamp switch must have a warning light to indicate to the driver when the lamps are switched on, and this switch must be wired in such a way that the rear fog lamp(s) cannot be used without either headlights, sidelights or front fog lamps also being on.

Any rear fog lamp fitted to a car manufactured from October 1, 1979 must also bear the appropriate 'E-mark' signifying conformity with EEC standards. If your car was manufactured prior to that date then you *need* not fit rear fog lamps at all; but if you do (and it obviously makes sense to do so) they must comply with the above regulations concerning positioning and independence of the brake lights.

Conditions requiring the use of rear fog lamps obviously also call for headlamps and/or front fog lamps. While front fog lamps may be used only in fog or falling snow, rear fog lamps are to be permitted in conditions of 'poor visibility' when only headlamps may be allowable at the front. It is suggested, therefore, that if you fit rear fog lamps they're wired using a relay, the actuating circuit of which is operated by the dipped headlamps circuit (ie the supply to teriminal 'W1' in our relay diagram would come from a dipped headlamp circuit connection).

The cable from the switch should be run through the car floor if possible and under the carpet, but don't forget to use grommets or the holes which you've drilled will cut through the cable insulation. An in-line fuse will be needed, probably about 10 amps rating, **93**

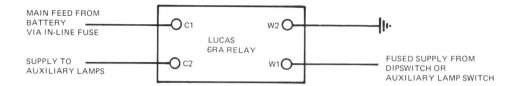

Connections for auxiliary lamps using a relay

but it will depend on the actual lamps fitted.

Anti-theft devices

There are three main categories of car thieves — those people who want your car either as a complete item or for the major mechanical and body parts; those who are out for a joy-ride; and those who merely want the contents. With any type of thief it makes sense to do what you can to deter someone from *wanting* to get in; don't leave valuables lying about, don't leave the car unlocked and, if it's parked at home, put it in a locked garage if possible. But, if a car thief decides he does want your particular car, statistically he's got a pretty good chance of getting it!

All Alpines and Solaras have a steering column lock which is a very effective protection against a car being driven away, but it still makes sense to have a good burglar alarm fitted. Many types are available, and many of these are wired into door courtesy light switches or hidden switches beneath seats. Other types are wired into the horn circuit, but separate horns and bells are available; the more unconventional it is (whilst still being reliable!) the better. Don't put hidden switches in the first place you think of — it might be the first place the thief thinks of too!

Some anti-theft devices are activated by the movement caused through somebody trying to get into the car (and occasionally by an innocent passer-by!). Some not only sound alarms, but also earth the ignition circuit; other devices simply mechanically lock together the steering wheel and clutch pedal. Have a look round the accessory shops and see what suits your car, your pocket and the degree of protection required.

A slightly different approach to the security problem is taken by manufacturers of kits containing the materials necessary to etch the car's registration number permanently onto each piece of window glass. This may be an effective deterrent against theft with re-use in mind, but it's no protection against the thief who only wants a joy-ride, or the professional who will strip the car of all its useful parts and leave the body (and windows!) dumped somewhere.

Radios and tape players

A radio or tape player's an expensive item to buy, and will only give its best performance if fitted properly. It's useless to expect concert hall performance from a unit that's suspended from the dash panel by string with its speaker resting on the back seat or parcel shelf! If you don't wish to do the installation yourself there are many in-car entertainment specialists who can do the fitting for you.

Make sure the unit purchased is the same polarity as the car (ie negative earth). Ensure that units with adjustable polarity are correctly set before commencing installation.

It's difficult to give specific information with regard to fitting. In any case, the unit will come with its own instructions. However, the following paragraphs give guidelines to follow, which are relevant to all installations.

Radios

Most radios are a standardised size of 7 inches wide, by 2 inches deep — this ensures that they'll fit into the radio aperture provided.

The type of aerial, and where you're going to fit it, is a matter of personal preference. In general, the taller the aerial, the better the reception but there are limits to what's practicable. If you can, fit a fully retractable type — it saves an awful lot of problems with vandals and car wash equipment. When choosing a suitable spot for the aerial, remember the following points:

(a) The aerial lead should be as short as possible
(b) The aerial should be mounted as far away from the distributor and HT leads as possible
(c) The part of the aerial which protrudes beneath the mounting point mustn't foul the road-wheels, or anything else
(d) If possible the aerial should be positioned so that the lead doesn't have to be routed through the engine compartment
(e) The aerial should be mounted at a more-or-less vertical angle

94

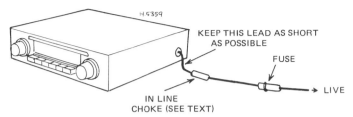

*An in-line choke should be fitted in the feed wire as
close to the unit as possible*

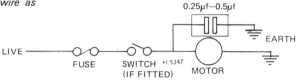

*The correct way to suppress electric motors which are
causing interference*

Radio interference suppression

Books have been written on the subject, so we're
not going to be able to tell you a lot in this small
space. To reduce the possibility of your radio picking
up unwanted interference, an in-line choke should be
fitted in the feed wire and the set itself must be
earthed really securely. The next step is to start
connecting capacitors to reduce the amount of
interference being generated by the different circuits
of the car's electrics. The illustrations show the
various interference generators and give capacitor
values for the suppressors. When it comes to the
ignition HT suppressors, these are resistors which can

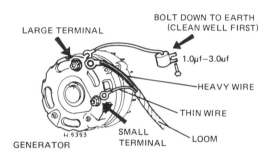

*How to connect a suppressor capacitor to the
alternator*

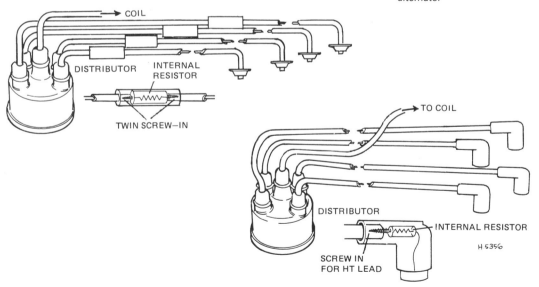

Ignition HT lead suppressors

either be suppressor-type plug caps or in-line suppressors; if you're already using resistive HT leads (those with the carbon fibre filling), they're already doing the job for you. They are standard equipment on new cars nowadays. Don't attempt any other means of suppressing ignition interference — it shouldn't be necessary with electronic ignition anyway, and you may damage expensive semiconductor components.

Tape players

Fitting instructions for both cartridge and cassette stereo tape players are the same and in general the same rules apply as when fitting a radio. Tape players aren't usually prone to electrical interference like radios — although it can occur — so positioning isn't so critical. If possible the player should be mounted on an even keel. Also, it must be possible for a driver wearing a seat belt to reach the unit in order to change or turn over tapes.

Visibility aids

Mirrors

Recent EEC legislation has done wonders for the looks of exterior mirrors. In addition to being functional, they now must have no projections to catch clothing or other cars, and must fold flat when struck. The result is a new wave of products in all shapes and sizes, some of which can be sprayed to match the existing car finish.

All models are fitted from new with at least a door mirror on the driver's side, whilst some are fitted with a mirror on each door. If you are thinking of changing the standard mirrors for any reason, choose mirrors which you think will suit the car's styling and, having got them, select the mounting point carefully. You'll get a good idea of where the best place is by simply looking at other cars, but get someone to hold the mirror while you sit in the driving seat just to make sure you can see all you need to.

Mark the position on the wing or door, and if you're fitting two mirrors do likewise on the other to make sure they're both in the same position. Check the hole size needed and, if you can, select a drill this size plus, where applicable, a smaller one to make a pilot hole. If you haven't got the large drill required for most wing mirrors, you'll have to drill several small holes and file them out to the correct size.

Don't forget to remove any burrs from the hole afterwards, then paint on a little primer to cover the bare metal edges. When the primer's dry you can fit the mirror following the maker's instructions, then **96** angle it as necessary to get the best rear view.

Comfort

Longer journeys can be much more pleasant if your car's comfortable to drive, and just a couple of suggestions on this theme may be welcome.

Sound reducing kits

Very few cars have yet been produced in which the noise level, particularly at motorway speeds, is all that could be desired. For economy reasons, most manufacturers put only a certain amount of underfelt and sound-deadening material into their cars, and a further improvement can usually be made by fitting one of the proprietory kits. These are usually tailored to fit individual models, and consist of sections of felt-like material which are glued in place under carpets, inside hollow sections etc, in accordance with instructions. The material can also be bought in rolls for DIY cutting, using the carpets etc as templates.

Seats

If your car seats are showing signs of old age (and just fitting new covers won't disguise the sagging when you sit in them) then you can of course have them rebuilt by an upholstery specialist. On the other hand you could think about replacing at least the driver's seat by one of the special bucket types available. To look at these you'll have to find an accessory shop stocking the more motor sports orientated kind of goods.

Miscellaneous

Roof racks

Many an owner has had to resort to a luggage rack from time to time, even if it's only for family holidays. The types available are very varied, but they normally rely on clips attached to the water drain channel above the doors. If you're buying, select a size that suits your requirements, making sure that it's not too wide for the roof!

When fitting the roof rack, position it squarely on the roof, preferably towards the front rather than the rear. After it's loaded, by the way, recheck the tension of the attachment bracket screws.

Don't overload the roof rack — 50 kg (110 lb) is the theoretical limit, but obviously the size of the load has to be considered as well as its weight. Take it easy on the corners when you've got a load lashed to the roof, and stop to check the security of the load after the first 50 miles or so.

Don't keep the roof rack on when it's not wanted; it offers too much wind resistance and creates a surprising amount of noise (see *Save It*!).

Mudflaps

You're probably already aware that both front and rear wheel arches can be fitted with mudflaps. These will not only protect your car's underside and paintwork from flying stones, but will also earn the thanks of following drivers owing to the reduction in spray during wet weather. Fitting's straightforward and is usually by means of clamping brackets or self-tapping screws.

Specialist fitments

We've now covered a lot of the main items likely to interest the average owner from the DIY fitting angle. Such things as towbars and sunshine or vinyl roofs, while practical or desirable, are beyond the scope both of this book and of the ordinary car owner. We therefore recommend that for any major accessory of this kind you consult the appropriate specialist who'll be able to give you an initial estimate of the cost as well as carrying out the work properly and safely.

Troubleshooting

We've gone to great lengths in this book to provide as much information on your car as we think you'll need for satisfactory running and servicing. Hopefully, you won't need to use this section but there's always a possibility (rather than a probability!) that something will go wrong, and by reference to the charts that follow you should be able to pinpoint the trouble even if you can't actually fix it yourself.

Before you even think about referring to the charts, though, it's worth asking yourself 'What was the last thing done to the car?' We're not insulting the standard of your work, just pointing out that it's ever so easy to knock a wire connector off when reaching for something deep in the engine bay, or to forget to tighten a loose clip when your assistant brings you a cup of tea.

The charts are broken down into the main systems of the car, and where there's a fairly straightforward remedy — the sort you can tackle yourself — **bold type** is used to highlight it. Further information on that particular item will normally be found elsewhere in the book; look up the particular component or system in the index to find the correct page. In some cases a reference number will be found (eg T1/1); by looking up this number in the accompanying cross-reference table, you'll find more information on that particular fault.

When confronted with a fault, try to think calmly and logically about the symptom(s), and you'll soon be able to work out what the fault *can't* be! Check or substitute one item at a time, otherwise when you do clear the fault you may not know exactly what was causing it. The commonest cause of difficulty in starting, especially in winter, is a poor spark at the plugs combined with a slow cranking speed from the starter motor. Make sure that your battery's kept fully charged, that the HT leads, coil and distributor cap are clean and dry, and that all connections are clean and tight. If all this is in order, then proceed with fault finding in other areas.

CROSS-REFERENCE TABLE

TROUBLESHOOTER REFERENCE	ADDITIONAL INFORMATION
T1/1	Either charge the battery from a battery charger, or use jump leads to start the car from another battery; make sure that the lead polarities are correct in both cases or you may do permanent damage.
T1/2	If the lead's loose, disconnect the battery earth lead, then tighten the connection on the starter motor. Reconnect the battery earth lead.
T1/3	Select 3rd gear (manual models only) and have a friend give you a push. As soon as you gather speed, let in the clutch. Drive to your dealer for (possibly) a new starter motor.
T1/4	Make sure all the connections are tight, then wipe the leads clean and dry with a lint-free cloth. Use an ignition system waterproofer (eg WD40 or Damp Start) to prevent it happening again if this is a regular problem with your car.
T1/5	An ignition coil is a simple item to fit, but make a note of the connections before removing them, and ensure that the replacement coil is the correct type.
T1/6	To check the operation of the pump, detach the fuel outlet pipe (that's the one that goes to the carburettor) and operate it by turning the engine over on the starter a few times. There should be a steady stream of petrol in spurts if the pump's working properly. Take care you don't spill fuel on the hot exhaust!

TROUBLESHOOTER REFERENCE	ADDITIONAL INFORMATION
T1/7	It's easy enough to tighten the attachment bolts if you've got a box or socket spanner of the right size.
T1/8	Wait till the system's cooled down, then top it up. If it happens a second time, get it looked at straight away or you could ruin your engine (if it hasn't happened already). If it's just a leaking water hose you can probably bind it up as in T2/2 to get yourself home.
T2/1	Driving carefully will probably get you home. An air line on the radiator core will clean out the dirt that's accumulated; if it's blocked internally, use a proprietary flushing compound.
T2/2	For a temporary repair a leaking water hose can normally be bound up with adhesive tape or, better still, with a hose bandage specially made for this purpose.
T2/2	Drive slower and don't labour the engine.
T4/1	You'll need a little extra pedal effort for braking but that's all. It may be possible to temporarily repair the vacuum hose as in T2/2.
T6/1	Remove the lamp lenses (see *In an Emergency*) and check for signs of rust. Where there's rust, scrape it off and apply a little petroleum jelly. Ensure that the screws securing the lamp body to the car are making good contact.

99

TROUBLESHOOTER 1:

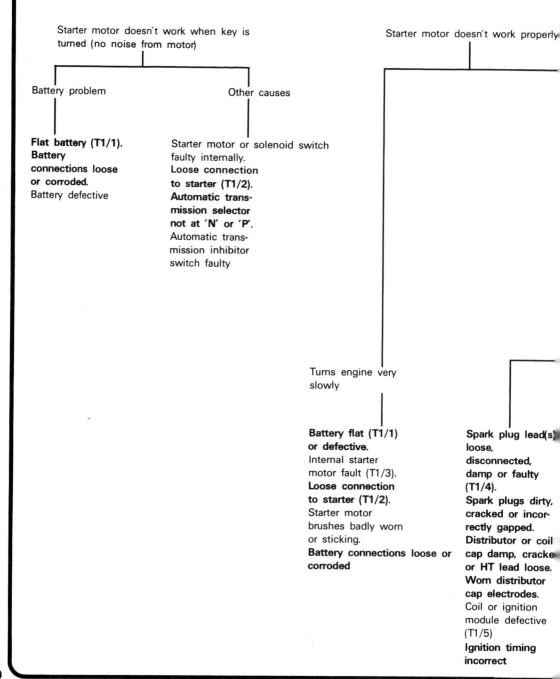

Starter motor doesn't work when key is turned (no noise from motor)

Battery problem

**Flat battery (T1/1).
Battery
connections loose
or corroded.**
Battery defective

Other causes

Starter motor or solenoid switch
faulty internally.
**Loose connection
to starter (T1/2).
Automatic trans-
mission selector
not at 'N' or 'P'.**
Automatic trans-
mission inhibitor
switch faulty

Starter motor doesn't work properly

Turns engine very
slowly

**Battery flat (T1/1)
or defective.**
Internal starter
motor fault (T1/3).
**Loose connection
to starter (T1/2).**
Starter motor
brushes badly worn
or sticking.
**Battery connections loose or
corroded**

**Spark plug lead(s)
loose,
disconnected,
damp or faulty
(T1/4).
Spark plugs dirty,
cracked or incor-
rectly gapped.
Distributor or coil
cap damp, cracke**
or HT lead loose.
**Worn distributor
cap electrodes.**
Coil or ignition
module defective
(T1/5)
**Ignition timing
incorrect**

ENGINE – STARTING

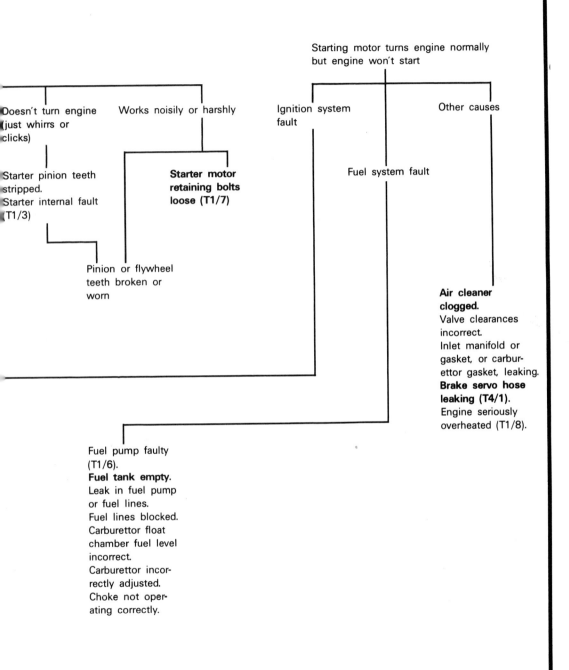

Starting motor turns engine normally but engine won't start

Doesn't turn engine (just whirrs or clicks)

Works noisily or harshly

Ignition system fault

Other causes

Starter pinion teeth stripped.
Starter internal fault (T1/3)

Starter motor retaining bolts loose (T1/7)

Fuel system fault

Pinion or flywheel teeth broken or worn

Air cleaner clogged.
Valve clearances incorrect.
Inlet manifold or gasket, or carburettor gasket, leaking.
Brake servo hose leaking (T4/1).
Engine seriously overheated (T1/8).

Fuel pump faulty (T1/6).
Fuel tank empty.
Leak in fuel pump or fuel lines.
Fuel lines blocked.
Carburettor float chamber fuel level incorrect.
Carburettor incorrectly adjusted.
Choke not operating correctly.

TROUBLESHOOTER 2:

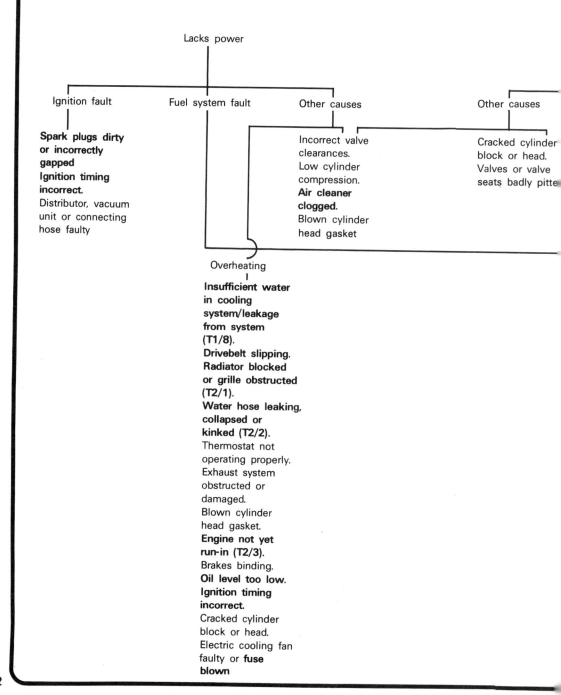

Lacks power

Ignition fault

**Spark plugs dirty
or incorrectly
gapped
Ignition timing
incorrect.**
Distributor, vacuum
unit or connecting
hose faulty

Fuel system fault

Other causes

Incorrect valve
clearances.
Low cylinder
compression.
**Air cleaner
clogged.**
Blown cylinder
head gasket

Other causes

Cracked cylinder
block or head.
Valves or valve
seats badly pitted

Overheating

**Insufficient water
in cooling
system/leakage
from system
(T1/8).
Drivebelt slipping.
Radiator blocked
or grille obstructed
(T2/1).
Water hose leaking,
collapsed or
kinked (T2/2).**
Thermostat not
operating properly.
Exhaust system
obstructed or
damaged.
Blown cylinder
head gasket.
**Engine not yet
run-in (T2/3).**
Brakes binding.
**Oil level too low.
Ignition timing
incorrect.**
Cracked cylinder
block or head.
Electric cooling fan
faulty or **fuse
blown**

ENGINE – RUNNING

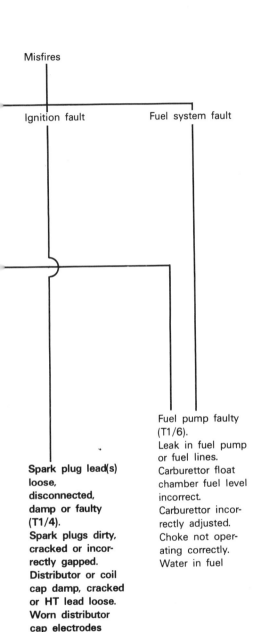

Misfires

Ignition fault   Fuel system fault

**Spark plug lead(s)
loose,
disconnected,
damp or faulty
(T1/4).
Spark plugs dirty,
cracked or incor-
rectly gapped.
Distributor or coil
cap damp, cracked
or HT lead loose.
Worn distributor
cap electrodes
Ignition timing
incorrect**

Fuel pump faulty
(T1/6).
Leak in fuel pump
or fuel lines.
Carburettor float
chamber fuel level
incorrect.
Carburettor incor-
rectly adjusted.
Choke not oper-
ating correctly.
Water in fuel

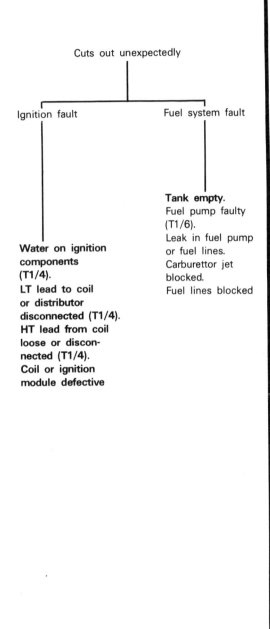

Cuts out unexpectedly

Ignition fault   Fuel system fault

**Water on ignition
components
(T1/4).
LT lead to coil
or distributor
disconnected (T1/4).
HT lead from coil
loose or discon-
nected (T1/4).
Coil or ignition
module defective**

**Tank empty.
Fuel pump faulty
(T1/6).
Leak in fuel pump
or fuel lines.
Carburettor jet
blocked.
Fuel lines blocked**

TROUBLESHOOTER 3:

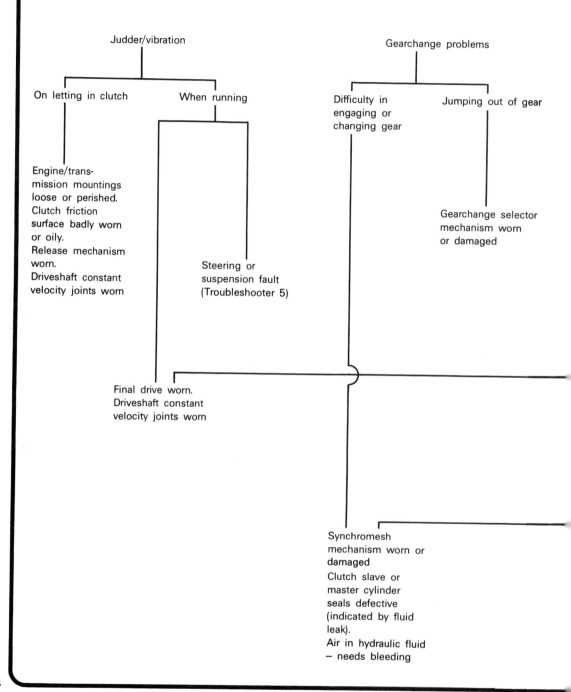

Judder/vibration

On letting in clutch

When running

Gearchange problems

Difficulty in engaging or changing gear

Jumping out of gear

Engine/trans-
mission mountings
loose or perished.
Clutch friction
surface badly worn
or oily.
Release mechanism
worn.
Driveshaft constant
velocity joints worn

Gearchange selector
mechanism worn
or damaged

Steering or
suspension fault
(Troubleshooter 5)

Final drive worn.
Driveshaft constant
velocity joints worn

Synchromesh
mechanism worn or
damaged
Clutch slave or
master cylinder
seals defective
(indicated by fluid
leak).
Air in hydraulic fluid
— needs bleeding

CLUTCH, GEARBOX AND FINAL DRIVE

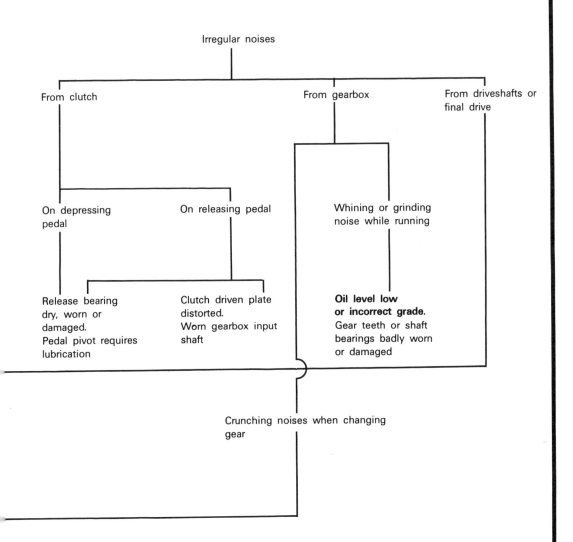

Irregular noises

From clutch

From gearbox

From driveshafts or final drive

On depressing pedal

On releasing pedal

Whining or grinding noise while running

Release bearing dry, worn or damaged.
Pedal pivot requires lubrication

Clutch driven plate distorted.
Worn gearbox input shaft

Oil level low or incorrect grade.
Gear teeth or shaft bearings badly worn or damaged

Crunching noises when changing gear

NOTE: Owing to the complexity of an automatic transmission unit, any fault diagnosis should be entrusted to your local dealer, who will have the necessary specialised equipment to test the unit.

TROUBLESHOOTER 4:

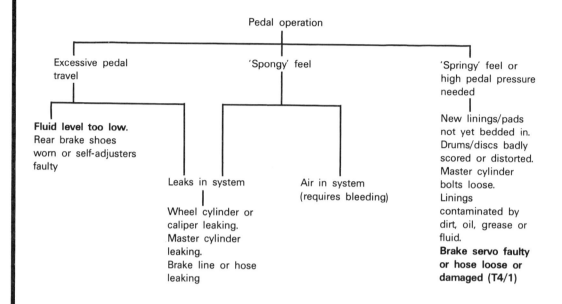

Pedal operation

Excessive pedal travel

Fluid level too low. Rear brake shoes worn or self-adjusters faulty

'Spongy' feel

Leaks in system

Wheel cylinder or caliper leaking. Master cylinder leaking. Brake line or hose leaking

Air in system (requires bleeding)

'Springy' feel or high pedal pressure needed

New linings/pads not yet bedded in. Drums/discs badly scored or distorted. Master cylinder bolts loose. Linings contaminated by dirt, oil, grease or fluid. **Brake servo faulty or hose loose or damaged (T4/1)**

TROUBLESHOOTER 5:

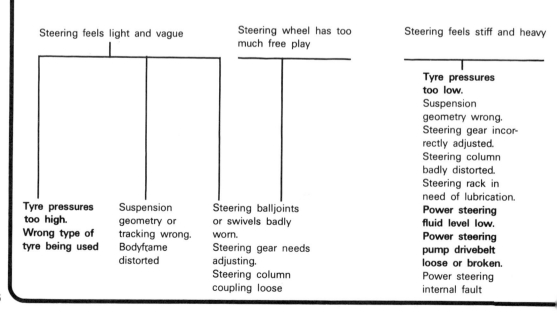

Steering feels light and vague

Tyre pressures too high. Wrong type of tyre being used

Suspension geometry or tracking wrong. Bodyframe distorted

Steering wheel has too much free play

Steering balljoints or swivels badly worn. Steering gear needs adjusting. Steering column coupling loose

Steering feels stiff and heavy

Tyre pressures too low. Suspension geometry wrong. Steering gear incorrectly adjusted. Steering column badly distorted. Steering rack in need of lubrication. **Power steering fluid level low. Power steering pump drivebelt loose or broken.** Power steering internal fault

BRAKES

Effect on car

Car pulls to one side

Tyre pressures unequal.
Drums/linings or pads/discs contaminated with oil, grease or fluid.
Brake backplate, caliper or disc loose.
Shoes or pads incorrectly fitted.
Differing types of linings fitted at each side.
Suspension anchorages loose.
Drums/discs badly worn or distorted

Brakes 'grab' or wheel(s) lock

Contamination by dirt, oil, grease or fluid.
Brake pressure regulating valve faulty

Brakes bind when pedal released

Handbrake over-adjusted.
Master cylinder pushrod out of adjustment.
Vent hole in reservoir cap blocked.
Master cylinder or wheel cylinder seized.
Broken or weak brake shoe return springs on rear brakes

STEERING/SUSPENSION

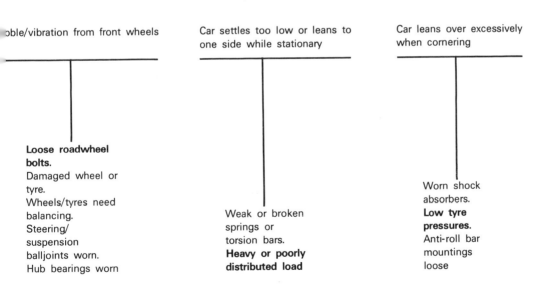

...oble/vibration from front wheels

Loose roadwheel bolts.
Damaged wheel or tyre.
Wheels/tyres need balancing.
Steering/ suspension balljoints worn.
Hub bearings worn

Car settles too low or leans to one side while stationary

Weak or broken springs or torsion bars.
Heavy or poorly distributed load

Car leans over excessively when cornering

Worn shock absorbers.
Low tyre pressures.
Anti-roll bar mountings loose

TROUBLESHOOTER 6:

NOTE: This chart assumes that the battery installed in your car is in good condition and is of the correct specification, and that the terminal connections are clean and tight. A car used frequently for stop-start motoring or for short journeys (particularly in winter when lights, heater blower etc are likely to be in use) may need its battery recharged at intervals to keep it serviceable. If an electrical problem occurs, don't immediately suspect the starter or any other component without first checking that the battery is capable of supplying its demands.

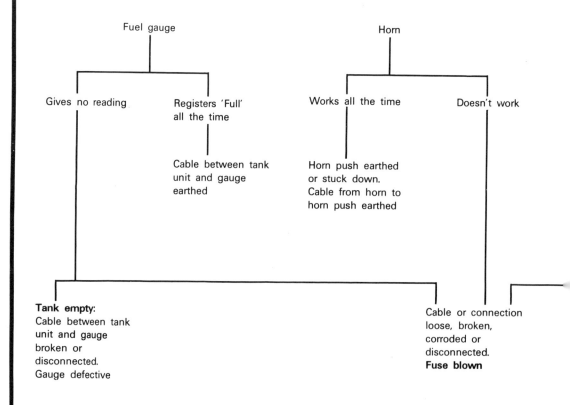

Fuel gauge

Gives no reading

Registers 'Full' all the time

Cable between tank unit and gauge earthed

Horn

Works all the time

Horn push earthed or stuck down. Cable from horn to horn push earthed

Doesn't work

Tank empty:
Cable between tank unit and gauge broken or disconnected.
Gauge defective

Cable or connection loose, broken, corroded or disconnected.
Fuse blown

A fault occurring in any other electrical equipment or accessory not specifically referred to can usually be traced to one of the three main causes, ie blown fuse; loose or broken connection to power supply or earth; or internal fault in the component concerned.

ELECTRICS

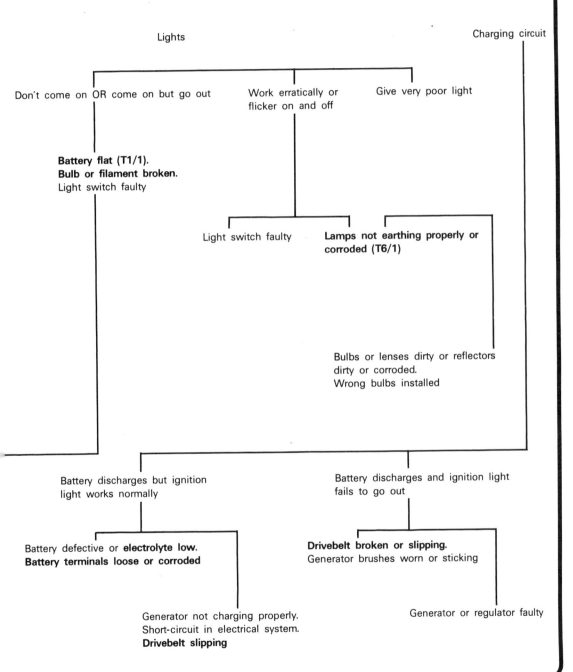

Lights

Charging circuit

Don't come on OR come on but go out

Work erratically or flicker on and off

Give very poor light

Battery flat (T1/1).
Bulb or filament broken.
Light switch faulty

Light switch faulty

Lamps not earthing properly or corroded (T6/1)

Bulbs or lenses dirty or reflectors dirty or corroded.
Wrong bulbs installed

Battery discharges but ignition light works normally

Battery discharges and ignition light fails to go out

Battery defective or **electrolyte low.**
Battery terminals loose or corroded

Drivebelt broken or slipping.
Generator brushes worn or sticking

Generator not charging properly.
Short-circuit in electrical system.
Drivebelt slipping

Generator or regulator faulty

Car Jargon Explained

We hope there isn't much in this Handbook that you can't understand. However, most of us – particularly if we're trying to learn more about an unfamiliar subject – will sooner or later come across the odd word or phrase that needs explaining. This alphabetical list should help you understand the language spoken by your garage man, 'expert' neighbour, or that inevitable chap in the local.

A

Accelerator pump: A device attached to many *carburettors* which adds a spurt of extra fuel to the carburettor mixture when the accelerator pedal is suddenly pressed down.

Additives: Compounds which are added to petrol and lubricating oil to improve their quality and performance.

Advance and retard: A system for altering the ignition timing – the time in the firing cycle at which the ignition spark occurs. The spark timing is normally a few degrees of *crankshaft* revolution before the *piston* reaches the top of its stroke, and is expressed as so many degrees before top-dead-centre (BTDC). It's altered by devices in the *distributor* which detect changes in engine speed and load. Broadly speaking, as the engine speeds up the ignition is advanced (greater angle BTDC) but if there is a heavy engine load the ignition is retarded (smaller angle BTDC).

AF: An abbreviation of 'across flats', the way in which many nuts, bolt heads and spanners are now identified. It's preceded by an Imperial or metric unit of measurement – eg ½ in AF or 11 mm AF.

Air cooling: Alternative method of engine cooling in which no water is used. An engine-driven fan forces air at high velocity over the engine surfaces, which are enclosed by cowling. Normally an *oil cooler* is incorporated in the air flow to assist the rate of heat loss.

Alternator: A device for converting rotating mechanical energy into electrical energy. In modern cars, it has superseded the *dynamo* for charging the battery because of its much greater efficiency.

Ammeter: A device for measuring the current supplied to the battery from the *dynamo* or *alternator,* or drawn from the battery by the car lights, wipers, radio etc.

Antifreeze: A chemical compound mixed with the cooling system water to lower the temperature at which the coolant freezes.

Anti-roll bar: A spring-steel bar mounted transversely across a car which counteracts the natural tendency for the car to lean over when cornering.

Aquaplaning: A phrase used to describe the action of a tyre skating across water.

Automatic transmission: A type of *gearbox* which selects the correct gear ratio automatically according to the engine speed and load.

B

Balljoint: A ball-and-socket type joint, used in *steering* and *suspension* systems, which permits relative movement in more than one plane.

Battery condition indicator: A voltmeter connected via the ignition switch to the car battery. Unlike an *ammeter* (which it's tending to supersede), it will warn you of impending battery failure.

Bearing: Metal or other hard wearing surface against which another part moves or rotates, and which is designed (and usually lubricated) to withstand the resulting friction.

Bendix drive: A device on many types of starter motor which allows the motor to be coupled to the *flywheel* for engine starting, then disengages when the engine commences to run.

BHP: See *Horsepower.*

Big end: The end of a *connecting rod* which is attached to the *crankshaft.* It incorporates a *bearing* and transmits the linear movement of the con-rod to the motion of the crankshaft.

Bleed nipple (or valve): A hollow screw with a tapered seat which allows air or fluid to be bled out of a system when it is loosened.

Brake caliper: That part of a *disc brake* system which houses the *brake pads* and the *hydraulic* operating *pistons.*

Brake fade: A temporary loss of braking efficiency due to overheating of the brake friction material.

Brake pad: That part of the *disc brake* system which comprises the friction material and a metal backing plate.

Brake shoe: That part of a *drum brake* system which comprises the friction material and a curved metal former.

Breather: A device which allows fresh air into a system or allows contaminated air out.

Bucket tappet: A cup (or bucket) shaped piece of metal used in some engines to transmit the rotary *camshaft* movement to an up-and-down movement for *valve* operation.

Bump stop: A hard rubber device used in many *suspension* systems to prevent the moving parts from lifting the bodyframe during violent suspension movements.

C

Camber angle: The angle at which the front wheels are set from the vertical, when viewed from the front of the car. Positive camber is the amount in degrees by which the wheels are tilted outwards at the top.

Cam follower: A cylindrical piece of metal used to transmit the rotary *camshaft* movement to an up-and-down movement for *valve* operation.

Camshaft: A rotating shaft with lobes or cams used to operate the engine *valves.*

Carbon fibre leads: Black, string-like cores in the centre of some spark plug *HT* leads, which don't need separate radio and *TV suppressors.*

Carburettor: A device which is used to mix air and fuel in the correct proportions for all conditions of engine running. There are two main types: those with a number of fixed *jets*, and those with a single jet with a moving needle in it. In the former type, the different jets come into operation at different conditions of throttle opening, engine speed and engine load; in the latter type, the *needle jet* is controlled by a

moving *piston*, the position of which depends on the amount of suction in the engine inlet *manifold.*

Castor angle: The angle between the front wheel pivot points and a vertical line when viewed from the side of the car. Positive castor is when the axis is inclined rearwards.

Centrifugal advance: System of ignition *advance and retard* incorporated in many *distributors* in which weights rotating on a shaft alter the ignition timing according to engine speed.

Choke: This has two common meanings. It is used to describe the device which shuts off some of the air in a *carburettor* during cold starting, and may be either manually or automatically operated. It's also used as a general term to describe the carburettor throttle bore.

Clutch: A friction device which allows two rotating devices to be coupled together smoothly, without the need for either rotating part to stop.

Coil spring: A spiral of spring steel used in many *suspension* systems.

Combustion chamber: Shaped area in the *cylinder head* into which the fuel/air mixture is compressed by the *piston* and in which combustion of the mixture is effected by the *spark plug.*

Compression ratio (CR): A term used to describe the amount by which the fuel/air mixture is compressed, and expressed as a number. For example, an 8.5 : 1 compression ratio means that the volume of fuel/air when the *piston* is at the bottom of its stroke is 8.5 times that when the piston is at the top of its stroke.

Compression tester: A special type of pressure gauge screwed into the *spark plug* hole which shows the *cylinder* compression when the engine is turning but not firing.

Condenser (capacitor): A device in the *distributor* which stores electrical energy and prevents excessive sparking at the *contact breaker* points.

Connecting rod: (con-rod): Rod in the engine connecting the *piston* to the *crankshaft.*

Constant velocity (CV) joint: A joint used in *driveshafts*, where the speed of the input shaft is exactly the same as the speed of the output shaft at any angle of rotation. This does not occur in ordinary *universal joints.*

Contact breaker: The device in the *distributor* which comprises the electrical points (or contacts) and a cam which opens and closes them to operate the *HT* electrical circuit which provides the spark at the *spark plug.*

Crossflow cylinder head: A *cylinder head* in which the inlet and exhaust *manifolds* are on opposite sides.

Crossply tyre: A tyre whose construction is such that the weave of the fabric material layers is running diagonally in alternately opposite directions to a line around the circumference.

111

Cubic capacity: The total volume within the *cylinders* which is swept by the *pistons*.

Cylinder head: That part of the engine which contains the *valves* and associated operating gear.

D

Damper: See *shock absorber*.

Dashpot: An oil-filled *cylinder* and *piston* used as a damping device in SU and Zenith/Stromberg CD type *carburettors*.

Dead axle (beam axle): The simplest form of axle, comprising a horizontal member attached to the chassis-frame by springs. This is used for the rear axle on some front-wheel-drive cars.

Decarbonizing ('decoking'): Removal of all carbon deposits from the *combustion chambers* of an engine.

De Dion axle: A rear axle comprising a cranked tube attached to the wheel hubs, with a separately mounted *differential* gear and *driveshafts*. Suspension is normally through *coil springs* between the wheel hubs and chassis frame.

Diaphragm: A stationary flexible membrane used in items such as fuel pumps. The diaphragm spring used in *clutches* is somewhat similar but is made from spring steel.

Diesel engine: An engine which relies upon the heat generated when compressing air to ignite the fuel, and which therefore doesn't need a *spark plug*. Diesel engines have much higher *compression ratios* than petrol engines, normally in the region of 20 : 1.

Differential: A system of gears (generally known as a crownwheel and pinion) which allows the *torque* from the *propeller shaft* to be applied to the driving wheels. The torque is divided proportionately between the driving wheels to permit one wheel to turn faster than the other if required, for example during cornering.

DIN: This stands for Deutsche Industrie Norm (roughly equivalent to the British Standards Institution) and lays down international standards for measuring output, performance, etc., of motor vehicles.

Disc Brakes: A braking system where a rotating disc is clamped between hydraulically operated friction pads.

Distributor: A collective term used to describe the *contact breaker, advance and retard* mechanisms, and associated parts of the *ignition system*.

Doughnut: A term used to describe the flexible rubber coupling used in some *driveshafts*.

Driveshaft: Name usually applied to the shaft (normally incorporating *universal* or *constant velocity* joints) which transmit the drive from a *transaxle* to

one wheel; more commonly found in front-wheel-drive cars.

Drive train: A collective term used to describe the *gearbox, propeller shaft, final drive* and *half-shafts* of a front engine/rear wheel drive car.

Drum brake: A brake with friction linings on 'shoes' running inside a cylindrical drum attached to the wheel.

Dual circuit brakes: A *hydraulic* braking system comprising two separate fluid circuits so that if one circuit becomes inoperative, braking power is still available from the other circuit at a reduced efficiency.

Dwell angle: The number of degrees of *distributor* cam rotation during which the *contact breaker* points are closed during the ignition cycle of one *cylinder*. The angle is altered by adjusting the points gap, and is a more accurate way of setting-up the *ignition system*.

Dynamo: A device for converting rotating mechanical energy into electrical energy. This is a heavier, less efficient form of *generator* than the *alternator* and has largely been superseded by it during recent years.

E

Earth strap: A flexible electrical connection between the battery and vehicle earth, or the engine/*gearbox* and chassis frame to provide the return current-flow path in the electrical system

Electrode: An electrical terminal or terminals, across which a spark occurs eg, in a *spark plug* or *distributor* cap.

Electrolyte: A current-conducting solution of water and sulphuric acid, which is the liquid inside the car battery.

Electronic ignition: An *ignition* system incorporating electronic components which can produce a much greater spark voltage than in conventional systems.

Emission control: The prevention or reduction of the emission into the atmosphere of noxious fumes and gases from the engine and fuel tank of a motor vehicle. Required to varying degrees by the laws of different countries, it is effected by design and by special devices.

Epicyclic gears (planetary gears): A gear system used in many *automatic transmissions* where there is a centre 'sun' wheel around which smaller 'planet' gears inside a 'planet carrier' route.

Exhaust gas analyser: An instrument used for the measurement of pollutants (mainly monoxide) in an exhaust system.

Expansion tank: A container used in many modern

cooling systems to collect the overflow from the car's *radiator* as the coolant heats up and expands.

F

Filter: A device for extracting foreign particles from air or oil.

Final drive: A collective term (often expressed as a gearing ratio) for the crownwheel and pinion (see *Differential*).

Flat engine: Form of engine design in which the *cylinders* are positioned horizontally, usually with an equal number each side of a central *crankshaft.*

Float chamber: That part of a *carburettor* which contains a float and *needle valve* for controlling the fuel level.

Flywheel: A heavy rotating disc attached to the *crankshaft* used to smooth out the pulsating output from the *cylinders.*

Four stroke (cycle): A common term used to describe the four operating strokes of a *piston* in a conventional car engine. These are: (1) Induction — drawing in the fuel/air mixture as the piston goes down; (2) Compression of the fuel/air mixture as the piston rises; (3) Power stroke where the piston is forced down after the fuel/air mixture has been ignited by the *spark plug* and (4) Exhaust stroke where the piston rises and pushes the burnt gases out of the *cylinder.* During these operations, the inlet and exhaust *valves* are opened and closed at the correct moment to allow the fuel/air mixture in, the exhaust gases out, or to provide a gas-tight compression chamber.

Fuel injection: A method of injecting fuel into an engine. Used in *Diesel* engines, and also on some petrol engines as a replacement for the *carburettor.*

G

Gasket: Compressible material used between two metal surfaces to make a leakproof joint.

Gearbox: A group of gears and shafts installed in a metal housing. Physically, this is positioned between the *clutch* and the *differential*, and is used to multiply the engine *torque.*

Generator: See *alternator* and *dynamo.*

H

Half-shaft: A rotating shaft, two of which are used to transmit the drive from the *differential* to the wheels.

Hardy-Spicer joint (Hooke's or Cardan joint): See *Universal joint.*

Helical gears: Gears in which the teeth are cut at a slant across the circumference to give smoother meshing and quieter running.

Horsepower: A measurement of the rate of doing work. Where brake horsepower (*BHP*) is referred to it's the amount of work required to stop a moving body.

HT: Abbreviation of high tension (meaning high voltage). Used in connection with the ignition system.

Hydraulic: A term used to describe the operation of a system by means of a fluid pressure.

I

Ignition system: The electrical system which provides the spark to ignite the air/fuel mixture in the engine. Normally it comprises the battery, ignition coil, *distributor, (contact breaker and condenser),* ignition switch, *spark plugs* and wiring.

Ignition timing: See *Advance and retard.*

Inertia reel: Automatic type of safety belt which permits the wearer to move freely in normal use but which locks to give restraint on sensing either sudden deceleration of the car or sudden movement of the wearer.

In-line engine: Engine in which the *cylinders* are positioned in one row as distinct from being e.g. a *flat* or *vee* formation.

J

Jet: A calibrated nozzle or orifice in a *carburettor* through which fuel is drawn for mixing with air.

Jump leads: Heavy electric cables fitted with clips to enable a vehicle's battery to be connected to an external one for emergency starting.

K

Kerb weight: The weight of a car, unladen but ready to be driven, i.e. with enough fuel, oil etc. to travel an arbitrary distance.

Kickdown: A device used on *automatic transmission* which allows a lower gear to be selected by flooring the accelerator.

Kingpin: A device which allows the front wheels of a car to swivel.

L

Laminated windscreen: A windscreen which has a thin plastic layer sandwiched between two layers of toughened glass. Its advantage is that it doesn't shatter or craze over when hit.

Leading shoe: Brake shoe of which the leading end (the one moved by the operating *cylinder*) is reached first by a given point on the drum during normal forward rotation. A simple single-cylinder *drum brake* will have one leading and one trailing (the opposite) shoe.

Leaf spring: A spring commonly used on cars with a *live axle*, comprising several long steel plates clamped together.

Little end: The smaller end of the *connecting rod* which is attached to the *piston*.

Live axle: An axle through which power is transmitted to the rear wheels.

Loom: A complete vehicle wiring system, or section thereof (e.g. front loom) comprising all the necessary cables of predetermined colours and lengths to wire up the various circuits.

LT: Abbreviation of low tension (meaning low voltage). Used in connection with *ignition* systems.

M

McPherson strut: An independent front *suspension* system where the swivelling, springing and shock absorbing action of the wheel is dealt with by a single assembly.

Manifold: The device used for ducting the air/fuel mixture to the engine (inlet manifold), or the exhaust gases from the engine (exhaust manifold).

Master cylinder: A cylinder containing a *piston* and hydraulic fluid, directly coupled to a foot pedal (e.g. brake or clutch *master cylinder*). It's used for transmitting pressure to the brake or *clutch* operating mechanism.

Metallic paint: Paint finish incorporating minute particles of metal to give added lustre to the colour.

Multigrade: Lubricating oil whose *viscosity* covers that of several *monograde* oils, making it suitable for use over a wider range of operating conditions.

N

Needle bearing: Type of *bearing* in which needle or cone-shaped rollers are employed around the inner circumference, often used to reduce the space needed for the bearing.

Needle valve: A component of the *carburettor* which restricts the flow of fuel or fuel/air mixture according to its position relative to an orifice or *jet.*

Negative earth: Electrical system (now almost universally adopted) in which the negative terminal of the car battery is connected to the vehicle body, the polarity of all other electrical equipment being determined by this.

O

Octane rating: A scale rating introduced by the British Standards Institution for grading petrol.

OHC (overhead cam): Describes an engine in which the *camshaft* is situated above the *cylinder head*, and operates the *valve* gear directly without the need for *pushrods.*

OHV (overhead valve): Describes an engine which has its *valves* in the *cylinder head* (as in *OHC*) but suggests that the valve gear is operated via *pushrods* from a *camshaft* situated lower in the engine. Practically all modern car engines are OHV but are not necessarily OHC.

Oil cooler: Small *radiator* fitted in the lubricating oil circuit and sited in a cooling airflow to dissipate heat from the oil. Used mainly in higher-performance engines.

Overdrive: A device coupled to a car *gearbox* which raises the output gear ratio above the normal 1 : 1 of top gear. Also used to describe a top gear ratio of greater than 1 : 1 found in some cars.

Oversteer: A tendency for a car to turn more tightly into a corner than intended.

P

PCV (Positive crankcase ventilation): A system which allows fumes and vapours which build up in the crankcase to be drawn into the engine for burning.

Pinion: A gear with a small number of teeth which meshes with one having a larger number of teeth.

Pinking: A metallic noise from the engine often caused by the *ignition timing* being too far advanced. The noise is the result of pressure waves which cause the cylinder walls to vibrate, when the ignited fuel/air is compressed.

Piston: Cylindrical component which slides in a closely-fitting metal tube or *cylinder* and transmits pressure. The pistons in an engine, for example, compress the fuel/air mixture, transmit the combustion power to the *crankshaft*, and exhaust the burnt gases.

Piston ring: Hardened metal ring which is a spring fit in a groove running round the *piston* to ensure a close fit to the *cylinder* wall.

Positive earth: The opposite of *negative earth.*

Propeller shaft: The shaft which transmits the drive from the *gearbox to the rear axle in front engine/rear drive.*

Pushrod: A rod which is moved up and down by the rotary motion of the *camshaft* and operates the rocker arm in an OHV engine.

Q

Quarter light: A triangular window often mounted in the front door of a car.

Quartz-halogen blub: A bulb with a quartz envelope (instead of glass) and a tungsten filament, and filled with one of the halogen group of gases (often iodine).

R

Rack and pinion: Simplest form of steering mechanism which uses a *pinion* gear to move a toothed rack.

Radial ply tyre: A type in which the tread plies are arranged laterally, at right angles to the circumferential plane.

Radiator: Cooling device, situated in an air flow and comprising a system of fine tubes and fins for rapid heat dissipation, through which engine coolant is passed.

Radius arms (rods): Locating arms sometimes used with a *live axle* to positively locate it in the fore-and-aft direction.

Recirculating ball steering: A derivation of *worm and nut* steering, where the steering shaft motion is transmitted to the steering linkage by balls running in the groove of worm gear.

Rev-counter: See *tachometer.*

Rocker arm: A lever which rocks on a central pivot, one end is moved up and down by the *camshaft* action and the other end operates the inlet or exhaust *valve.*

Rotor arm: A rotating arm in the *distributor* which distributes the *HT* spark voltage to the correct *spark plug.*

Running on: A tendency for an engine to keep on running after the ignition has been switched off; it's often caused by badly maintained engine, or use of an unsuitable grade of fuel.

S

SAE: Society of Automotive Engineers (of America). The SAE classification of oils is well known but, as with *DIN* standards, SAE covers a wide range of measuring output, performance, etc, of motor vehicles.

Safety rim: A special wheel rim shape which prevents a deflated tyre from rolling off the wheel.

Sealed beam: A sealed headlamp unit where the filament is an integral part and cannot be renewed separately. Although much more expensive than separate bulbs, the illumination does not deteriorate due to contamination.

Semi-elliptic spring: A *leaf spring* used for many car rear *suspension* systems.

Semi-trailing arm: A common form of independent rear *suspension* which allows the wheel carrier to be pivoted.

Servo: A device for multiplying the normal effort applied to a control. With a brake servo, this uses the suction created in the engine inlet *manifold* to act on a *diaphragm/pushrod* for additional braking effort; it's attached to the brake *hydraulic master cylinder.*

Shock absorber: A device for damping out the up-and-down movement of a car when the *suspension* hits a bump in the road.

Sonic-idle carburettor: A *carburettor* where the air used for the fuel/air mixture at idle speeds is mixed in a special by-pass tube which increases the pressure drop. The velocity of the mixture increases to above the speed of sound and at the same time it becomes very turbulent which improves the fuel/air atomization.

Spark plug: A device with a ceramic insulator and two electrodes on a common metal body which screws part-way into the engine *combustion chamber.* When the *HT* voltage is applied to the plug terminal, a spark jumps the air-gap at the electrodes.

Squab: Another name for a seat cushion.

Steel-braced tyre: Tyre in which an extra ply containing steel cords is incorporated to give added strength.

Steering arm (knuckle): Short arm on the rear face of **115**

the front *stub axle* to which the steering linkage connects.

Steering rack: See *Rack and pinion*.

Stroboscopic light: A light powered from the engine *ignition system* which is used for checking the ignition timing when the engine is running (i.e. dynamically).

Stroke: The total travel of the *piston* in the bore.

Stub axle: A short axle which carries the wheel only.

Sub-frame: A small frame or chassis which carries the *suspension*, and which in turn is connected to the car body.

Sump: The main oil container at the lowest part of an engine.

Suppressor: A device which is used to suppress or damp-out electrical interference caused by the *ignition system* or *generator*, wiper motor etc.

Suspension: A general term used to describe the links, springs and *dampers* with which the car body is suspended on the wheels.

Swing axle: A *suspension* arm which is pivoted near the centre-line of the car, and which gives the wheel a vertical swinging action about the pivot point.

Synchromesh: A device in a *gearbox* which synchronizes the speed of one gear shaft with another to produce smooth, noiseless engagement of the relative gears.

T

Tachometer: Also known as a rev counter, this indicates the engine speed in revolutions per minute (rpm).

Tappet: A term nowadays widely misused to refer to the adjustable part of the valvegear of an engine. True tappets are found only in the valvegear of older engines.

Thermostat: A device which is sensitive to changes in engine termperature, and opens up an additional path for coolant to flow when the engine has warmed up.

Tie-rod (track rod): A general term for a rod which provides location for a component, or between two components (as with steering linkage).

Timing chain: Metal flexible-link chain engaging on sprocket wheels and driving the *camshaft* from the *crankshaft* in an *OHV* engine.

Timing marks: Mark normally found on the *crankshaft* pulley or *flywheel* and used for setting the ignition firing point with respect to a particular *piston*.

Toe-in/toe-out: The amount by which the front wheels point inwards or outwards, expressed either as an angle or linear measurement.

116 **Top dead centre (tdc):** The point at which a piston is at

the top of its stroke.

Torque: The turning effort generated by any rotating part.

Torque converter: A coupling where the driving *torque* is transmitted through oil. At low speeds there is very little transference of torque from the input to the output; as the input shaft speed increases, the direction of fluid flow within a system of vanes alters and torque from the input impeller is transferred to the output turbine. The higher the input speed, the closer the output speed approaches it, until they are virtually the same.

Torsion bar: A spring-steel bar which turns about its own axis, and is used in some independent front *suspension* systems.

Toughened windscreen: A windscreen which will shatter in a particular way to produce blunt-edged fragments or will craze over but remain intact. A zone-toughened windscreen has a zone in front of the driver which crazes into larger parts to reduce the loss of visibility which occurs with toughened windscreens, but is otherwise similar.

Track rod: A rod which connects the steering arms to the steering gear and/or steering idler gear.

Trailing arm: A form of independent *suspension* where the wheel is attached to a swinging arm, and is mounted to the rear of the arm pivot.

Transaxle: A form of combined *gearbox* and axle from which two shafts transmit the drive to the wheels.

Transmission: A general term for a *gearbox*, but very often used as an alternative for a *transaxle*.

Two-stroke (cycle): A common term used to describe the operation of an engine where each downward piston stroke is a power stroke. The fuel/air mixture is ported into the crankcase where it's compressed by the descending *piston* and 'pumped' through another port into the *combustion chamber*. As the piston rises, the mixture is compressed and ignited, which forces the piston down. The burnt gases flow from the exhaust port, but the piston is now compressing a further charge in the crankcase which repeats the cycle. The engine needs careful design to prevent the unburnt and burnt gases from mixing and, although not a feature of the simplest designs, in some versions a rotary or reed *valve* is incorporated to help achieve this.

U

Understeer: A tendency for a car to go straight on when turned into a corner.

Universal joint: A joint that can swivel in any direction whilst at the same time transmiting *torque*. It's commonly used in *propeller shafts* and *driveshafts*, but is not suitable for some applications because the input and output shaft speeds are not the same at all positions of angular rotation. The type in common use is known as a *Hardy-Spicer*, Hooke's or Cardan joint.

Unsprung weight: That part of a car which is not supported by the springs.

Upper cylinder lubricant (UCL): A type of light oil intended to be added to a car's fuel with the object of providing extra lubrication for the *cylinder* walls.

V

Vacuum advance: System of ignition *advance* and *retard* used in certain *distributors* where the vacuum in the engine intake *manifold* is transmitted to the distributor and acts on a *diaphragm* to alter the ignition timing according to throttle position.

Vacuum gauge: A device which indicates the amount of vacuum or suction in the inlet *manifold*.

Valve: A device which opens or closes to permit or stop gas flow into the engine.

Vee engine: Design in which the *cylinders* or an engine are set in two banks forming a V when viewed from one end. A V8, for example, consists of two such rows of four cylinders each.

Venturi: A streamlined restriction in the *carburettor* throttle bore which causes a low pressure to occur; this sucks fuel into the air stream to form a vapour suitable for combustion.

Viscosity: A term used to describe the resistance of a fluid to flow. When associated with lubricating oil it's given an *SAE* number, 10 being a very light oil and 140 being a very heavy oil.

Voltage regulator: A device which regulates the *generator* output to a predetermined level. For most *alternator* systems this is an integral part of the alternator itself, and therefore mainly applicable to *dynamo* systems. Regulators on later cars also have a device to regulate the charging current as well as the voltage.

W

Wankel engine: A rotary engine originally developed by Felix Wankel which has a triangular shaped rotor in an epitrochoidal housing (approximate in shape to a broad-waisted figure of eight). The engine has never proved popular in production cars in the UK.

Wheel balancing: Adding weights at the rim of a car wheel so that there are no out-of-balance forces.

Wishbone: An A-shaped *suspension* link, pivoted at the base of the A, and carrying a wheel at the apex. Normally mounted in an approximately horizontal plane.

Worm and nut steering: A steering system where the lower end of the steering column has a coarse screw thread on which a nut runs. The nut is attached to a spindle which carried the drop arm which, in turn, moves the steering linkage.

CONVERSION

Distance

Inches (in)	X	25.400	= Millimetres (mm)
Feet (ft)	X	0.305	= Metres (m)
Miles	X	1.609	= Kilometres (km)
Millimetres (mm)	X	0.039	= Inches (in)
Metres (m)	X	3.281	= Feet (ft)
Kilometres (km)	X	0.621	= Miles

Capacity

Inches, cubic (cu in/in^3)	X	16.387	= Centimetres, cubic (cc/cm^3)
Fluid ounce, imperial (fl oz)	X	35.51	= Centimetres, cubic (cc/cm^3)
Fluid ounce, US (fl oz)	X	29.57	= Centimetres, cubic (cc/cm^3)
Pints, imperial (imp pt)	X	0.568	= Litres (L)
Quarts, imperial (imp qt)	X	1.1365	= Litres (L)
Quarts, imperial (imp qt)	X	1.201	= Quart, US (US qt)
Quarts, US (US qt)	X	0.9463	= Litres (L)
Quarts, US (US qt)	X	0.8326	= Quarts, imperial (imp qt)
Gallons, imperial (imp gal)	X	4.546	= Litres (L)
Gallons, imperial (imp gal)	X	1.201	= Gallons, US (US gal)
Gallons, US (US gal)	X	3.7853	= Litres (L)
Gallons, US (US gal)	X	0.8326	= Gallons, imperial (imp gal)
Centimetres, cubic (cc/cm^3)	X	0.061	= Inches, cubic (cu in/in^3)
Centimetres, cubic (cc/cm^3)	X	0.02816	= Fluid ounces, imperial (fl oz)
Centimeters, cubic (cc/cm^3)	X	0.03381	= Fluid ounces, US (fl oz)
Litres (L)	X	28.16	= Fluid ounces, imperial (fl oz)
Litres (L)	X	33.81	= Fluid ounces, US (fl oz)
Litres (L)	X	1.760	= Pints, imperial (imp pt)
Litres (L)	X	0.8799	= Quarts, imperial (imp qt)
Litres (L)	X	1.0567	= Quarts, US (US qt)
Litres (L)	X	0.220	= Gallons, imperial (imp gal)
Litres (L)	X	0.264	= Gallons, US (US gal)

Area

Inches, square (in^2/sq in)	X	645.160	= Millimetres, square (mm^2/sq mm)
Feet, square (ft^2/sq ft)	X	0.093	= Metres, square (m^2/sq m)
Millimetres, square (mm^2/sq mm)	X	0.002	= Inches, square (in^2/sq in)
Metres, square (m^2/sq m)	X	10.764	= Feet square (ft^2/sq ft)

Weight

Ounces (oz)	X	28.350	= Grammes (g)
Pounds (lbs)	X	0.454	= Kilogrammes (kg)
Grammes (g)	X	0.035	= Ounces (oz)
Kilogrammes (kg)	X	2.205	= Pounds (lbs)
Kilogrammes (kg)	X	35.274	= Ounces (oz)

FACTORS

Pressure

Pounds/sq in (psi/lb/sq in/ lb/in^2)	X 0.070	= Kilogrammes/sq cm (kg/sq cm)
Pounds/sq in (psi/lb/sq in/ lb/in^2)	X 0.068	= Atmospheres (atm)
Kilogrammes sq cm (kg/sq cm)	X 14.223	= Pounds/sq in (psi/lb/sq in/ lb/in^2)
Atmospheres (atm)	X 14.696	= Pounds/sq in (psi/lb/sq in/ lb/in^2)

Torque

Pound - inches (lbf in)	X 0.0115	= Kilogramme - metres (kgf m)
Pound - inches (lbf in)	X 0.0833	= Pound - feet (lbf ft)
Pound - feet (lbf ft)	X 12	= Pound - inches (lbf in)
Pound - feet (lbf ft)	X 0.138	= Kilogramme - metres (kgf m)
Pound - feet (lbf ft)	X 1.356	= Newton - metres (Nm)
Kilogramme - metres (kgf m)	X 86.796	= Pound - inches (lbf in)
Kilogramme - metres (kgf m)	X 7.233	= Pound - feet (lbf ft)
Newton - metres (Nm)	X. 0.738	= Pound - feet (lbf ft)
Newton - metres (Nm)	X 0.102	= Kilogramme - metres (kgf m)

Speed

Miles - hour (mph)	X 1.609	= Kilometres - hour (kph)
Feet - second	X 0.305	= Metres - second (m/s)
Kilometres - hour (kph)	X 0.621	= Miles - hour (mph)
Metres - second (m/s)	X 3.281	= Feet - second
Metres - second (m/s)	X 3.600	= Kilometres - hour (kph)

Consumption

Miles - gallon, imperial (mpg)	X 0.354	= Kilometres - litre (km/l)
Kilometres - litre (km/l)	X 2.825	= Miles - gallon, imperial (mpg)

Temperature

Centigrade (^{o}C) to Fahrenheit (^{o}F)

$$\frac{9}{5}\,^{o}C + 32 = {^{o}F}$$

Fahrenheit (^{o}F) to Centigrade (^{o}C)

$$\frac{5}{9}\,(^{o}F - 32) = {^{o}C}$$

Index

A

Accessories 89
Acknowledgements 2
Additives 37
Air cleaner –
   seasonal setting check 80
Air filter –
   element renewal 78
   housing cleaning 57
Air horns 92
Alternator drivebelt –
   checking/adjusting 57
Anti-theft devices 94
Automatic transmission 17
Automatic transmission fluid –
   changing 80
   level check 62
Auxiliary instruments 89
Auxiliary lights 93

B

Battery –
   buying 38
   condition indicator 89
   electrolyte level check 55
   terminal cleaning 61
Body –
   filling and spraying 85
   maintenance 69, 81, 83
   paintwork 84
   pinstripes 88
   repair 86, 87
   rust holes and gashes 85
   upholstery painting 88
Brakes –
   fault diagnosis 106, 107
   fluid level check 55
   handbrake adjustment 77
   maintenance 80
   pad inspection for wear 63
   pad wear light and test switch 16
   pipes and flexible hoses inspection 63
   pressure regulating valve check 73
   servo air filter renewal 79
   shoes inspection for wear 73
   warning light 14
Breakdown roadside 27
Bulb renewal –
   direction indicator (front) 31
   headlamps 30
   instrument panel light 32
   interior light 32
   rear light 31
   sidelamp 31

C

Cable renewal –
 choke 34
 handbrake 34
 speedometer 34
 throttle 33
Carburettor –
 idle adjustment check 72
Child safety seats and harnesses 92
Choke –
 cable 34
 warning light 14
Clock 90
Clutch fault diagnosis 104, 105
Consoles 91
Controls lubrication of 61
Conversion tables 118, 119
Coolant level checking 23, 53
Cooling fan operation check 56
Cooling system check 82
Crankcase breather flame trap cleaning 79

D

Direction indicator –
 bulb (front) 31
 flasher renewal 33
 switch 16
Driveshaft gaiters inspection 63
Driving habits 36

E

Economy devices 36
Electrical failures 29
Electrical system fault diagnosis 108, 109
Engine fault diagnosis 100 to 103
Engine oil –
 dipstick calibration 23
 grade 23
 level check 53
 renewal 56
 topping-up 23
Exhaust systems, buying 38

F

Final drive fault diagnosis 104, 105
Fog lights 93

Fuel –
 gauge 14
 in-line fuel filter renewal 79
 octane rating 25, 37
 pump filter cleaning 71
 tank capacity 25

G

Garages self-service 24
Gearbox fault diagnosis 104, 105

H

Handbrake –
 adjustment 77
 cable 34
Hazard warning switch 16
Headlamps –
 beam alignment 31
 bulb renewal 30
Heated rear window switch 16
History of model range 8
HT components check 59

I

Ignition switch/steering lock 15
Ignition timing check 71
Instrument panel –
 gauges 11
 light 32
 warning lights 14
Insurance 38
Interior light 32

J

Jacking-up and wheel changing 28

L

Lighting/horn switch 15
Lights –
 auxiliary 93
 check 56, 81
 fog 93
 spot 93

INDEX

Lights maintenance of –
   direction indicators (front) 31
   direction indicators flasher 33
   headlamps 30, 31
   instrument panel 32
   interior 32
   rear 31
   sidelamps 31
Low fuel warning light 15
Lubricant and fluids 37

M

Maintenance 36
Manual gearbox/final drive oil change 78
Mirrors 96
Mudflaps 97

N

No charge warning light 15

O

Oil filter renewal 69
Oil pressure gauge 14, 90
Oil pressure/oil level warning light 14

P

Performance figures 10
Power steering drivebelt and fluid level check 59

R

Radios 94, 95
Rear fog lamps switch 16
Rear hub bearings lubrication 79
Rear light 31
Road test after service 69
Road test data 10
Roof racks 96
Routine maintenance 51

S

Safety 52
Seats 96

Servicing –
   schedules 53
   seasonal 80
Shock absorbers and mountings inspection 63
Sidelamps 31
Sound reducing kits 96
Spare parts buying 38, 39
Spares and repairs kit 26
Spark plugs 59, 60, 71
Specifications –
   automatic transmission 44
   braking system 45
   clutch 44
   cooling system 41
   dimensions and weights, general 47
   driveshafts 45
   electrical system 46
   engine 41
   final drive 45
   fuel system 43
   ignition system 43
   manual gearbox 44
   steering 45
   suspension 45
   tyres 46
   wheels 46
Speedometer –
   cable 34
   general 11
Spot lamps 93
Steering –
   fault diagnosis 106, 107
   rack gaiters inspection 63
Suspension, fault diagnosis 106, 107
Switches –
   direction indicator 16
   facia 16
   ignition/steering lock 15
   lighting/horn 15
   other 16
   windscreen wiper/washer control 15

T

Tachometer 14, 90
Tape players 96
Technical specifications see **Specifications**
Technical terms 110
Temperature gauge 14
Throttle cable 33
Timing ignition 71
Tools 49, 51
Towing and being towed 34
Transmission oil level check 61

Troubleshooting –
brakes 106, 107
clutch, gearbox and final drive 104, 105
electrics 108, 109
engine 100 to 103
steering/suspension 106, 107
use of charts 98
Tyre pressures –
checking 22, 56
recommended 25
Tyres, buying 38

V

Vacuum gauge 91
Valve clearances checking and adjusting 70

Vehicle identification numbers 39
Voltmeter 14

W

Warning devices 92
Warning lights –
brake 14
choke 14
low fuel 15
no charge 15
oil pressure/oil level 14
Wheel bolts tightness check 69
Wheel changing 28
Windscreen and tailgate washer levels check 55
Windscreen wiper/washer control 15